The Nearly-wed Handbook

THE NEARLY-WED HANDBOOK

How to Survive

the Happiest Day of Your Life

Dan Zevin

AVON BOOKS  NEW YORK

AVON BOOKS, INC.
1350 Avenue of the Americas
New York, New York 10019

Copyright © 1998 by Dan Zevin
Visit our website at http://www.AvonBooks.com
ISBN: 0-380-97555-6

Zevin, Dan.
    The nearly-wed handbook : how to survive the happiest day of your life / Dan
Zevin.—1st ed.
        p.   cm.
    1. Weddings—United States—Planning.   2. Mate selection—Humor.
I. Title.
HQ745.Z48   1998   97-52302
395.2'2—dc21   CIP

First Avon Books Printing: June 1998

To Megan,
who is in no way related
to the fictional case-study bride, "Peg,"
depicted in these pages.

Acknowledgments

A mushy, all-purpose thank-you note goes out to: Virginia Barber, Mary Ellen Bavaro, Stephanie Booth, Sari Boren, Hal Cantor, Tyler Clements, Esther Crain, Cindy Eagan, Erin Flynn, Jennifer Hershey, Sophia (Merunka) Lamberson, Adam Lichtenstein, Claudia Logan, Kevin MacRae, Tia Maggini, Jay Mandel, Peter Mann, Megan Paterson-Brown, Lisa Pierpont, Chris Radant, Ian Ruderman, Jennifer Rudolph-Walsh, Lithe Sebesta, Sara Shaw, Erica Stanley, Keith Summa, Megan Tingley, Claire Tisne, Allyson Zevin, and my caffeine caretakers at The Someday Cafe.

Contents

The Nearly-wed Handbook

Introduction

I Now Pronounce You Nearly-weds

You knew something was screwy from the start. There were no awkward silences on the first date. No signs of psychopathology on the second. And by the third date, you were struck with a revelation: *"We are actually having a third date."*

Yep, you had to admit there was a connection here. Not one of those forced, *kind of* connections like with that last loser ("Well, I never thought I'd marry someone with three nostrils and a crack habit, but we both really like eggs . . ."), but a genuine one. You liked the same music, the same books, the same films. Maybe you didn't always *love* the same music, books, and films, but that was okay. You loved hearing each other explain *why* you didn't always love the same music, books, and films. Half the time you weren't listening anyway. You were just sitting there, mesmerized by the way each other's lips moved, absorbed in deep, meaningful thoughts such as: "I believe I could watch this person's lips move for the rest of my life."

It was all very weird. You stopped noticing attractive members of the opposite sex. You started referring to yourself as "we." Once, when you heard the Carpenters' rendition of "We've Only Just Begun" on your K-Tell *Super-Cheesy Hits of the Seventies* CD, you caught yourself singing along. "This is a really good song," you were actually heard saying. From there, it was just a matter of time.

Okay, so maybe it didn't happen quite this way for you. Maybe the two of you got engaged five minutes after your first date. Maybe you waited five years after signing your first lease. Maybe you're going to be deported to a foreign country unless you secure a green card within the next five minutes. But regardless of your background, something deep inside of you changes the moment you set forth on that path to weddinged bliss.

You lie awake each night pondering the Big Questions: "Sit-down or buffet?" "Cash bar or open bar?" "Band or DJ?" You develop a remarkable new ability to tell the difference between embossed, engraved, and thermographic offset-printed envelopes. You become enrolled in swing dancing lessons. You're a Nearly-wed now! And from this day forward, for better or for worse, you're going to devote yourself to a single, all-consuming commitment: a commitment to planning The Happiest Day of Your Life.

Think of it! Your nearest and dearest are going to come from all over, bearing gifts from Crate & Barrel. Photographers are going to trail you. Musicians are going to serenade you. Caterers are going to feed you. YOU, my friend, are going to have your own *florist*. Everything's going to be perfect. Even if it kills you.

Meet fictional case study Nearly-weds "Stan" and "Peg," who are in no way based upon me, Dan, or my lovely nonfictional bride, Meg. When Stan and Peg decided they were ready to tie the knot, they thought they knew exactly what kind of wedding they wanted. After all, they'd been living in sin for years, which gave them plenty of time to spend every weekend of every spring of every year attending the weddings of all their friends. In their capacity as professional guests, they'd seen it all, from generic McCeremonies to Cinderella-style extravaganzas that lasted all week, and once involved the release of two hundred mourning doves.

But Stan and Peg were determined to have a more personal wedding—a wedding that would reflect their relationship. Something with a sense of substance, of balance, of fun. And as they set out to plan this profoundly meaningful event together, they learned something very important about each other: Neither of them had a clue what they were doing.

Not that there was any shortage of experts. Wedding guidebooks, most of which were very pink and apparently penned sometime before the women's suffrage movement, laid down the laws in no uncertain terms: "When planning a small gathering for fewer than eight hundred on a Saturday before six o'clock, it would be a *faux pas* of irrevocable proportions for the bride's parasol to be festooned with anything but miniature sweetheart chrysanthemums." Then their parents started getting into the act. "You *must* get Incredible Wedibles to do the catering," Peg's mother insisted. "Whatever you do, do *not* get Incredible Wedibles to do the catering," Stan's mother urged.

Tugged in a trillion different directions, Peg—a woman, it should be noted, who owns four (4) briefcases—found herself developing a disturbing new dependency on periodicals with names like *Bashful Bride-to-Be*. Stan would find her flipping through the glossy pages late at night, fantasizing about the genetically superior couples who were always being whisked off by horse-drawn carriage to some perfect little chapel overlooking the Mediterranean Sea. "Twenty-four pounds," Peg would whisper, tearing out a page and taping it to her bathroom scale. "Twenty-four pounds and that gown will be mine."

To Stan, it seemed like some mysterious "inner bride" was taking hold of Peg. An inner bride who, deep down, wanted everything to be as perfect as a *Bashful Bride* photo spread. An inner bride who would never, under any circumstances, festoon her parasol with anything but miniature sweetheart chrysanthemums. An inner bride who once provoked Peg and Stan to have a heated argument—to actually *raise their voices*—over the incendiary issue of linen patterns.

It was then, in a blinding moment of clarity, that they were finally struck with the fundamental truth of the Nearly-wed experience: *Getting married is entirely different from getting weddinged.*

GETTING MARRIED	GETTING WEDDINGED
You publicly declare your love in front of the people who mean the most to you.	You desperately revise your guest list according to which of these people are worth the seventy-five bucks a head it's costing to feed them.
You make the most mature, adult decision of your life.	You spend three hours deciding whether to register for the sterling silver olive pitter or the crystal margarita decanter with cactus-theme swizzle sticks.
You want to spend each and every moment together.	You spend each and every moment together trying to figure out which table senile Uncle Abe should sit at.
You make a profound commitment to the single most important person in your life.	You put down a deposit on a professional wedding planner.

As you enter into your new lives as Nearly-weds, remember: To have a successful marriage, all you need is trust, respect, and an undying commitment to the person you love enough to stick with forever. To have a successful *wedding*, though, you need something *really* hard to sustain:

a sense of humor. Keep that in mind and you'll not only *survive* the Happiest Day of Your Life, you just might enjoy it.

Take it from "Stan and Peg."

Engaged to Be Nearly-wed

How to Get Yourself Committed

....

The Marriage Proposal

In ancient times[1] the marriage proposal was an impetuous, romantic gesture in which the gentleman asked, the lady consented, and they both wound up in custody court twenty years later. Today's Nearly-weds mustn't be so hasty. Even if you've been dreaming of the big day since preschool, it's best to preface the marriage proposal with the marriage *pre-posal*. The standard pre-posal takes just three years:

The Marriage Pre-Posal
(Year One)

Live together for at least ten months without allowing the M word to pass your lips. Toward the end of month eleven,

[1]when our parents got married

wonder if you have a fear of commitment. Decide that you don't, but your partner does. Relieved, allow another month for partner to work problem out.

When parents or other interrogators ask if you ever plan to wed, issue the following reply: "We're *nothing* like all those mundane married couples who need a piece of paper to validate their love." Overlook the fact that renting movies every weekend, going to bed by ten-fifteen every night, and never seeing your friends anymore[2] makes you *exactly* like all those mundane married couples who need a piece of paper to validate their love.

Year Two

Sometime in June—or the day after you attend the wedding of a child you used to baby-sit for—begin acknowledging the possibility that yes, perhaps maybe one day you two may eventually think about getting married, sometime—potentially. Break up temporarily because you "need more space."

Year Three

Pop the questions. At a mutually agreed-upon date, time, and place, pose the following hypothetical queries: If we

[2]except for brunch

ever got married, when would we do it? Where would we do it? Who would we invite? Where will they sit? What will we serve? How many children will we have? What will their names be? What about their middle names? What colleges will they go to? Who will get custody of them in twenty years? Etc.

After each of these queries has been addressed, the gentleman is expected to surprise and startle the lady by popping the real question: "So ya want a ring?"

A Groom's Guide to Ring Wrangling

After the groom is overcome with the most romantic impulse he has ever experienced—the longing to share his life with his one true love—the next step is attaching a dollar value to that love. Is she worth $10,000? $5,000? $12.99 a month in six E-Z payments for the Angela Lansbury *Faux* Garnet Flake spinning around on QVC?

Grooms, get hold of yourselves! We're talking about a woman you love more than anyone you've ever loved before. A woman who fulfills and completes you. A woman who, if you're lucky, has a very wealthy mother who has waited her whole life to pass the family diamond down to her favorite daughter.

And even so, you'll *still* be moved to scour the world over in your search for the perfect ring . . .

Where to Find the Perfect Ring

The best place to go shopping for a ring is the place your fiancée has told you to go. Make sure to bring the accordion file she has given you containing . . .

1. the place's address and telephone number
2. the precise circumference of her finger
3. the topographic map she has drawn leading you to the correct display case
4. the stack of Polaroids she has taken of the ring she has selected

You may also want to take along any ring you might have purchased from QVC in an unenlightened moment. Trade it in for something of equal value, such as a piece of wrapping paper.

Jewelers: Modern Servants of Satan?

If your fiancée isn't the "hinting" type, you'll have to find a jeweler by yourself. Most large cities have a designated "jewelry district." You'll know you've arrived in this district because the merchants will be sporting a stylish array of headgear, such as yarmulkes, turbans, and authentic Mafiaso-style fedoras. If your community doesn't have a jewelry district, choose a professional jeweler you can trust, such as one who has completed his or her parole term. Also, make sure all jewelers you consider have several framed diplomas certifying that they've attended Jewel School. It is only there that they learn the techniques necessary to sell you a ring:

(A) THE GUILT TECHNIQUE

GROOM: Can you tell me something about this ring over here?

PROFESSIONAL JEWELER: Oh, yes, that's a very popular style, especially now that it's prom season and the boys are all looking for a "starter ring" to impress their little sweethearts. Of course, the rule of thumb for a man *your* age is to spend two years of your annual adjusted gross income on something she won't be ashamed to wear in public. But who am I to judge? If you don't love her, you don't love her.

(B) THE CONFUSION TECHNIQUE

GROOM: Can you tell me something about this ring over here?

PROFESSIONAL JEWELER: As you can see, the marquise cut is faceted to maximize the solitaire crown, and the eighteen-karat solid gold silver setting on the fourteen-volt dip-switch jumper pin is rated PG13 with a Vo2 max of thirty-three gigabits, six cylinders, and a woodsy, fruity bouquet typical of the Noire Valley region of Peru. If you loved her, you'd get her something more expensive.

GROOM: Can you tell me something about this ring over here?

PROFESSIONAL JEWELER: We are having a one-day-only sale on that baby right here, right now, just today! You are not going to find a ring of that quality at that price anywhere, ever, for as long as you live. That ring will only be on sale for five more minutes. If you do not buy that ring within the next four minutes and fifty-eight seconds, a better groom will beat you to it—a groom who loves his fiancée far more than you do. You have three more minutes. Act now or your marriage will be doomed.

How to Rate a Ring

After studying the dizzying variety of engagement rings, one thing will be clear to the Nearly-wed groom: They all look exactly the same, just like wedding gowns and children. That's why most grooms ultimately find themselves judging rings according to "the four Cs." The four Cs are: **cost, cost, cost** and **cost** (see opposite).

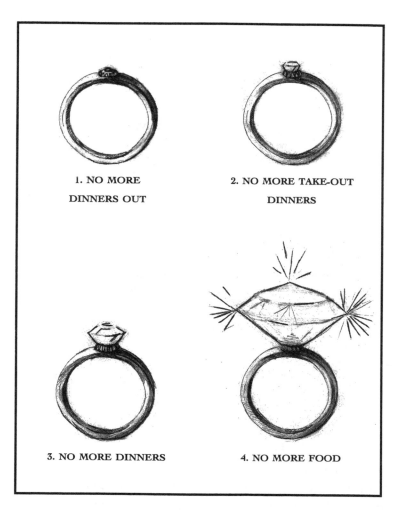

1. NO MORE DINNERS OUT

2. NO MORE TAKE-OUT DINNERS

3. NO MORE DINNERS

4. NO MORE FOOD

The Bridal Consultation

Before any of you grooms actually buy the ring you've chosen, I urge you to get a second opinion. This opinion should come from your fiancée. Why? Because, in her opinion, she hates the ring you have chosen.

WHAT SHE SAYS: Oh. That is a nice ring, honey.
WHAT SHE MEANS: That is the most hideous piece of flotsam I have ever seen.

Guys, don't be insulted just because your fiancée says you chose a "nice" ring. Instead, go shopping *together* until she finds one she likes.

WHAT SHE SAYS: Oh. This is a nice ring, honey.
WHAT SHE MEANS: GET ME THIS RING OR I AM PACKING MY BAGS, PAL.

A Bride's Guide to Ring Receiving

It is the bride's responsibility to make believe she has no idea that she's about to become the recipient of an engagement ring. A candlelit dinner for two on the Ritz-Carlton roof deck? Nothing out of the ordinary! A Valentine's Day flight to Paris on a chartered Learjet? So what else is new!

Backstage passes to Oprah's show on "Guys Who Lose Their Girlfriends by Proposing on Daytime TV?" Who knew??

Of course, there are some times when it's easier to act surprised than others. During a romantic night out on the town, your Romeo just might hide the ring in your flute of sparkling wine or conceal it beneath the parsley of your seared tuna. Imagine how surprised you'll be when you find it lodged inside your trachea as you become "breathless with emotion!"

NEARLY-WED BRIDE: I am so surprised! Where did you ever find such an exquisite ring?!

NEARLY-WED GROOM: What are you talking about? It's the one you told me to get.

N.B.: I love it!

N.G.: And I love you. Will you marry me?

The Proposalette

In this age of equal rights, a woman shouldn't wait around for some lazy, unmotivated boyfriend to pop the question. She should break up with him before he ever gets the chance. As for gals who *are* interested in wedding their present paramours, there are many ways for a would-be bride to say, "Will you marry me?" Here are some of the most popular:

- Offering to do his laundry = "Will you marry me?"

- Peeing with the door open = "Will you marry me?"

- Asking him to go to Baby Gap with you = "Will you marry me, sire my children, not leave me for a buxom twenty-two-year-old as soon as I reach menopause, and retire with me to a condominium complex in Arizona where you'll spend your golden years playing bingo and attending senior–citizen––discount matinees with me?"

Going Public

....

How to Tell Your Parents

What could be more thrilling than getting both sets of parents together, unscrewing some champagne, and announcing: "Mom, Dad, we're getting mm . . . mmm . . . *married!*" Yet it's not always possible to do this in person, particularly when (a) the two sets of parents live on opposite sides of the country or (b) the two sets of parents have remarried into four, six, and eight sets of parents. To simplify matters, I recommend conducting a group conference call. That way you can hang up on all your parents at once when the conversation proceeds as follows:

BRIDE: The reason we've conference-called you all here today is because we've got some big news.
BRIDE'S MOTHER: You're having a baby?
GROOM: No, we're getting married!

GROOM'S MOTHER: Wonderful! Who's gonna do my hair?

BRIDE'S STEPMOTHER: When is it? We can't have it in July. We have tickets to *Phantom* in July.

GROOM'S FIRST STEPFATHER: Where's the reception? Let's have it at the country club. Okay, it's settled.

BRIDE'S SECOND STEPFATHER: The country club?! Cousin Phinneus went to a wedding there and said it was drafty. We'll have it at the Sheraton.

GROOM'S THIRD STEPMOTHER: If we're having it at the Sheraton, it has to be during the day. Aunt Minnie won't drive after dark.

GROOM'S FIRST STEPMOTHER: Uncle Ira has bursitis.

GROOM'S FATHER: Claudia Stamish hates the swing music.

BRIDE'S FATHER: Look, kids, you two do whatever you want and just tell me how much you need. What is it, a hundred dollars? One fifteen? Hey, a wedding is a once-in-a-lifetime experience.

BRIDE'S FATHER'S FIRST WIFE: Ha! If it was a once-in-a-lifetime experience for *you*, maybe you'd have more than a hundred bucks to spend on your own kid's wedding!

BRIDE'S FATHER'S SECOND WIFE: Well, maybe if he didn't have to shell out alimony to *you* every month, there'd *be* money left over for the wedding!

GROOM'S MOTHER'S BOYFRIEND: Excuse me, but the people no one is talking about here are—

GROOM'S FATHER'S BOYFRIEND: The florists!

BRIDE'S MOTHER: No poinsettias. Mrs. Norton has a phobia.

BRIDE'S FATHER: The *Nortons* are coming? If the Nortons are coming, we can't invite the Zellinskis. Don't you remember that Thanksgiving they stormed out after the wishbone incident?

GROOM'S MOTHER: Speaking of Thanksgiving, now that you two kids are getting married, we thought you'd have the holidays with *us* every year, agreed? Kids? Are you there? Hello??

(AWKWARD THREE-SECOND PAUSE)

BRIDE'S MOTHER: Oh well, bad connection. So anyway, what should we do for hors d'oeuvres? I'm thinking we'll have pasta stations . . .

Informing Your "Friends"

Two things you can count on when breaking the news to friends: (1) Some friends will shout, "I'll be there!" and offer to throw you parties, buy you presents, and help plan the wedding. (2) Most of these friends are work friends, friends of friends, and assorted semifriends you weren't planning to invite to the wedding. As for your *real* friends, expect the following reactions to the statement "By the way, we're getting married."

THE BLANK STARE

Typically rendered by longtime single friends, this vacant gaze lasts approximately five seconds, during which time stricken parties review their entire lives in comparison to yours, wonder if *they* are ever going to get married, worry that you will never call them again after *you* get married, recall that time you beat them in the tetherball tournament at Splashy Pond Day Camp, feel insanely jealous over the fact that everything has always come so easily to you while they will probably end up miserable and alone like one of those hunchback mall-walkers from the senior center, feel like a terrible person for thinking this way because they really *are* glad for you, sob uncontrollably, and mutter: "Congratulations, I couldn't be happier."

The Delirium

"HIP, HIP, HOORAY!" they scream in gleeful unison. "Now you'll be just like us!" A classic reaction of the recently espoused, evangelical joy is a trademark of couples who plan to relive their wedding through yours. "First, you'll come to dinner and we'll show you all our pictures. Then we'll make your guest list and find your florist, and when we get back from your honeymoon, we'll all move in together and bear each other's children!"

The Position Statement

"Oh, you're getting married?" they condescend. "That's fine for some people, but we feel it's an archaic institution that not only discriminates against gays, lesbians, and the rare Cape Verdian white-tailed platypus, but ultimately signifies a selling out of one's personal freedom to a patriarchal culture that rewards blind conformity to some secular humanist notion of gender politics." Nine months later, these people are married, living in Connecticut, and planning the PTA lawn darts tournament.

THE BEST FRIEND BLESSING

Female version: "Oh my God!! I can't believe you're getting married!"
Male version: "Oh my *God*. I can't believe you're getting *married*."

An Engagement Party Primer

The purpose of an engagement party is to practice introducing the person formerly known as your boyfriend or girlfriend as: *my fiancé*. "Hello, this is MY FIANCÉ," you should say to your guests, trying not to crack up over the fact that you actually have one. "MY FIANCÉ is very pleased to meet you, too, aren't you, FIANCÉ? Yes, you and MY FIANCÉ certainly have a lot in common. Goodbye, and I'm so glad you had a chance to meet MY FIANCÉ here at our engagement party. See you at the wedding!"

Sometime after announcing your betrothal to each individual in the Western world, it is customary for one of you to flip out, barricade yourself in the bedroom with a remote control and a sleeve of Fig Newtons, and declare that you're not ready to go through with it.

This time-honored ritual is an indication to friends and family that the wedding arrangements are proceeding in a perfectly normal fashion. I urge you to get this rite of passage out of your system early on, before you're bound by a deep sense of commitment.[3] Besides, promptly breaking the engagement leaves plenty of time to break it several more times before the wedding, offering a welcome respite from the pressures of planning. To make it official, contact your local newspaper, and instead of placing another boring engagement announcement, try publishing . . .

---

[3]fifty percent up front to the caterers, stationers, musicians, etc.

The Estrangement Announcement

Ben and Rhonda Shtingley are delighted to announce the estrangement of their daughter, Peg, and her fiancé, Stan. The couple were estranged after Stan staggered home following a weekend bender with one of his still single buddies, who regaled him with tales of bachelorhood involving a pair of Finnish twins, a can of Reddi-wip, and the question: "So, Stan, how does it feel to know you're never going to have sex with anyone but Peg for the rest of your life?" Upon arriving home with the stench of Jaegermeister on his breath, the groom found his bride enmeshed in another ugly telephone call with her dear mother, who merely called to remind her that the olive dress she chose for the rehearsal dinner makes her look like "anemic Aunt Moina." When the groom agreed, the bride burst into tears and hurled her diamond ring at him with a force powerful enough to inflict a mild concussion. Upon snapping back to reality, the visibly shaken Stan issued a heartfelt apology, confessing that he couldn't bear to lose the most important person in his life, and adding that Peg's rehearsal-dinner dress makes her look "hotter than a pair of Finnish twins slathered in Reddi-wip." It was at this point that the bride removed the barricade from her door, put away the remote control, and offered her betrothed a conciliatory Fig Newton. The couple plans to wed sometime in the spring.

Postproposal Priorities

Once you've decided to really go through with it, a whirl-wind of planning awaits. There's ordering the invitations, choosing the menu, finding the subsidized housing unit your parents will move into once they're released from debtors' prison, etc.

Before getting sidetracked with such trivia, tackle the only task worthy of your immediate attention . . .

Registering for Gifts

....

Pinch Us, We're Dreaming

How would you respond if I told you that right now you could waltz into any number of your favorite department stores and pick out absolutely whatever you wanted to get you started in your new life as happily married adults? How would you respond if I told you that you wouldn't have to pay for *any* of this stuff, and that it would all be brought forth in fancy gift-wrapped boxes? How would you respond if I told you that this utopian vision actually *exists*, and that it is known in the Nearly-wed lexicon as "registering"? If you're like most Nearly-weds you'd respond like this:

Typical Bride Response to Registering

"Matching dishes. We're definitely signing up for those cool blue plates from Crate & Barrel. And Polo bedsheets. Do you have any idea how sick I am of sleeping on that Holly Hobby pillowcase I've had since I used to wear a retainer? We're going to be *married* people! We're going to get a set of forks that don't have the ValuJet logo on them! And champagne glasses. Don't you *love* those tulip ones in the Domestications catalog? Hey, I just remembered! Williams Sonoma has that awesome KitchenAid Mixer—Master thing I've been wanting. Hmmm, I wonder what you do with one of those things . . ."

Typical Groom Response to Registering

"Home Depot is open till ten o'clock on Thursday nights."

Typical Couple Response to Registering

Most Nearly-weds resolve to register together at a mutually agreed-upon store, such as any store of the bride's choosing. This helps the groom learn his place in the wedding-planning process right off the bat.

First, you stand around in a heavy-volume bottlenecking delay of other Nearly-weds who've chosen to register together at a mutually agreed-upon store. You'll know you're in the right line if the couples gradually transform into seething single women standing all alone while their supportive future spouses are off in the Porch-'n-Patio department scarfing down free samples of charbroiled elk sausage.

Once you get to the front of the line, you are greeted by a "registry consultant," or "cyborg," who has been programmed to congratulate you repeatedly as you fill out reams of questionnaires regarding your lifestyle, average household income, whether you've ever heard voices in your head telling you to "drown the dolly," etc. Upon completion, your address is beamed via satellite to mailing lists throughout the solar system, explaining why, three days after registering, you'll start getting letters to the effect of: "Dear Bride and Groom, have you considered the advantages of celebrating your special day at the Museum of Cardboard Boxes?"

Your cyborg's duties also include providing a ballpoint pen, a printout of the store's inventory, and a handsome clipboard which may turn out to be your first gift, depending on the store's security system. As the two of you skip through the aisles signing up for such must-haves as SKU #002-V(ii): *Ceramic cream-soup tureen with chafing dish,* use your pen to take notes on each selection. "What is a cream-soup tureen with chafing dish?" you might write, for example. It may help to know that the majority of options on wedding registries have something to do with the preparation, presentation, and consumption of: foodstuffs. This explains why so many couples get fat after they get married.

What You Can Register For

Food-related or not, your choices fall into three categories:

  Category 1. Things You Already Have.
  Category 2. Things You Don't Need.
  Category 3. Bowls.

It is truly astounding how many bowls are available to the registered Nearly-weds. There are salad bowls and casserole bowls; gold-gilded bisque bowls and hand-painted fruit-ripening bowls; deep bowls, shallow bowls, bowls to hold other bowls; and horrible, herniating crystal bowls that serve no purpose whatsoever except to say to the world: "*We* are married." Certain Nearly-weds[4] receive so many bowls that they have to buy a special wrought-iron bowl rack to hold them all. But to afford the rack, they have to sell all the bowls. Then what do they have? A bowl

---

[4] e.g. "Stan," "Peg"

rack with no bowls in it. As we see, it makes little sense to register for anything in Category 3.

It makes even less sense to register for anything in Category 1 (Things You Already Have), mainly because most of these things came from garage sales and won't be worth much when you attempt to return them for cash.

The obvious solution is to sign up only for things you don't need (Category 2). Why? Because by the end of your shopping spree, a couple of little voices—the voices of your inner bride and groom—are going to convince you both that you really *do* need these things.

This is exactly what happened to fictional case-study Nearly-weds "Stan" and "Peg," who are in no way based on me, Dan, and my lovely, nonfictional bride, Meg. After spending three (3) hours scouring through stemware, hollowware, inner-, outer-, and underwear, all Stan and Peg had actually registered for was a set of glass lager steins (Stan's choice), and a pair of flannel pillowcases (Peg's choice). Finally, out of the corner of their eyes, they spotted a take-charge couple of Nearly-weds over in seafoodwares—a couple who, incidentally, brought their *own* clipboard with them to the store—registering for a scary-looking metal cage.

"Excuse me," Peg asked them sheepishly. "What is that?"

"It is a bluefish poacher," replied the other Nearly-weds, kindly sparing her the phrase "duh."

"Of course! A bluefish poacher!" Peg exclaimed, furiously checking it off on her clipboad. "We, too, enjoy poached bluefish, and how often we've yearned to poach it ourselves instead of relying upon others to do our poaching for us!" It was all downhill from there. In their registration frenzy, Stan and Peg also decided they needed the heat-retaining Pizza Stone, the tropical-fish napkin rings, and a set of much-needed highball glasses they didn't need.

I suggest you do the same, as all of this is excellent practice for selecting the two necessities you *especially* don't need . . .

The China Syndrome

When registering for china, be sure to bring your mother, since (a) she is the one forcing you to register for china, and (b) if she doesn't go, you'll be trailed by a squadron of spinsterish sales help who'll suspect you are trying to shoplift one of their Ppfaltzhengråffhn gravy boats. Remember, these ladies haven't left the china shop since the French and Indian War, and still believe you must choose a china pattern to match the estate you'll be buying after the honeymoon. When they peer down at you through their trifocals and ask, "What is your color scheme?" answer with confidence: "I am Caucasian and my fiancé is black." This will scare them off pronto, and you'll be free to select a pattern that's right for *you*.[5]

---

[5]Author's suggestion: "Paper by Dixie," reinforced with wax coating to prevent greasy soak-through.

Skip the Silver

It is a known Nearly-wed fact that couples who register for good silver never use it. This is because no one can afford to buy them enough to use. Result: After examining, inspecting, and trying to figure out how to eat with an endless array of overpriced flatwear, most couples wind up with one set of tarnished serving tongs that Grandma Belle and twelve of her canasta partners chipped in for with the last of their Social Security savings.

If *you* are in the market for more than one eating utensil, there's no shame in registering for plain old stainless steel. Especially if you store it in a velvet-lined walnut box from Tiffany.

Why it Pays to Register

One good reason to register is that it saves your guests trouble. Instead of searching all over town to get you those perfect pewter egg cups, they just go to the stores where you've registered, criticize everything you've chosen, and get you something they decide is much more "you."[6] Another good reason to register is that it allows you to return all your gifts for a full cash refund. Simply follow this convenient money-laundering guide:

[6]such as a chromium-plated lemon zester

Many Happy Returns

STORE	GIFT YOU REGISTER FOR	GIFT YOU RECEIVE	HOW TO RETURN GIFT FOR CASH
• Bloomingdale's	• Ralph Lauren extra-plush "bath sheets"	• earthenware mixing bowl	• claim bowl was a "duplicate" gift; receive bank check in two weeks
• Crate & Barrel	• standing barbecue grill	• wicker and porcelain inner/outer chips-'n-dip bowl	• place bowl in "Bloomies" shopping bag; bring to Bloomingdale's, follow instructions above
• Williams Sonoma	• All-clad cookware set	• painted pasta bowls (rooster motif)	• accidentally hurl bowls off rooftop, notify UPS that they arrived "damaged"
• Macy's	• Bluefish poacher	• Bluefish poacher	• blame "inner bride"

Nontraditional Nearly-weds often register at offbeat places like record stores or sporting goods shops to help relatives and friends get them things they actually want. This is preposterous. The majority of your relatives have no intention of getting you the latest Butthole Surfers boxed set, and the majority of your friends have no intention of getting you anything.

If a nontraditional registry is what you want, eschew the offbeat and embrace the practical. Send the following checklist to your guests at least five months before your wedding, and who knows? You may even get something you can use.

The Nearly-weds' Exclusive,
Reality-Based Gift Registry

Formal Kitchenware
> half-and-half
> sponges (two-sided)
> Hefty bags
> twisty ties
> Diet Coke (twelve-ounce cans)
> maid (live-in)

Electronics Equipment
> duct tape
> extension cords (six-hundred)
> speaker wire

Bathware
> Lysol Basin, Tub, and Tile Cleaner (advanced
>   scrubbing bubbles formula)
> toilet paper (two-ply)
> floss (waxed)
> ibuprofen (vat of)

The Bride's Trousseau
> hand cream
> mustache bleach
> personal dry-cleaning machinery

The Groom's Trousseau
> nose hair clippers
> underwear without holes in it
> WD40

Home Essentials
> down payment
> mortgage

Nearly-wed
Fundamentals

Blurry Visions

....

What's _Your_ Wedding Fantasy?

Before the real planning can start, you should create a vision of a wedding that reflects your personalities, just as your parents have already created an image of a wedding that reflects _their_ personalities. Maybe you're both "outdoorsy," and you imagine a wedding in which your whole family — even Great-grandma Ida with the detachable legs — snowshoes up a cliff for the ceremony and hang-glides down to the reception below. Maybe you're both "artsy," and you dream of creating everything yourselves, from the invitations to the centerpieces to the wine you'll make by stomping on grapes in your bathtub. Or maybe you're both "employed," and you envision the headaches and painful bleeding ulcers that go into pulling off a wedding while holding down a job.

What's _your_ wedding fantasy? Use the guide that follows to begin your process of elimination:

I. The Tacky Spectacular

This wedding unfolds in a Knights of Columbus hall festooned with mirrored disco balls, pink streamers, and crepe paper wedding bells that say "Tiffany ♥ Sal 4ever!" Like the bridesmaids' hair, everything in sight must be big and shiny—the gold spray-painted carnations; the powder blue, polysynth tuxedos; the groom. But the crowning jewel is the all-frosting, twelve-story wedding cake, adorned with marzipan Roman pillars and a battery-operated Asti Spumanti fountain spewing from the horn of a candy-coated unicorn perched atop the penthouse tier. Once the couple shoves a slice into each other's faces, *huzzah!* The Tony Cheesetone All-Bald Wedding Combo strikes up alternating renditions of "The Macarena" and the theme from *Ice Castles*. The day concludes as the bride and groom[7] grab their doggie bags and depart for their Poconos honeymoon in a white '78 Trans Am, as some of the guests throw glitter, some throw confetti, and some throw up.

II. The Granola Gathering

Held at sunrise on a favorite beach, farm, or endangered Amazonian rain forest, *this* Happiest Day begins when ten guests—many of whom are dogs with bandannas on them—form a circle and hum the couple down the aisle to the tune of "I'd Like to Teach the World to Sing." Emerg-

[7]and the videographer

ing through a smoke cloud of ceremonial patchouli incense, the love birds skip barefoot into the circle's center—the bride wearing a traditional Nigerian dashiki and holding a bouquet of pesticide-free salad greens; the groom in tie-dyed Tibetan robes and a garland of psilocybin mushrooms crowning his (blond) dreadlocks. The reception starts after a naked shaman healer/massage therapist pronounces them "persons of love," and peaks with a colorful group hallucination, sign-interpreted for the hearing-impaired.

III. THE UNDERSTATED AFFAIR

This Happiest Day allows everyone to act as old as their families' money, so anything too showy (*especially* emotions) is shunned. The wedding is held in a simple, appropriate chapel at noon, the bride in Mummy's debutante gown and pearls; the groom in Granddad Argyle's morning coat and ascot. At 12:01 the guests—strictly family and a few of the couple's most attractive friends from Exeter lacrosse and Junior League—will gather at the golf club for a luncheon of cucumber finger sandwiches daintily cut into equilateral triangles, and lovely stale crumpets for dessert. Of course, they won't overdo it by serving *enough* food, since no one would dream of disturbing the lovely presentation by eating any of it—especially since their congenital lockjaw prevents them from ingesting solids. Instead, they'll sip colossal quantities of champagne (Moet, 1615), emboldening them to engage in a round of synchronized ballroom dance and hush-toned gossip regarding cousin Corky's scandalous hem length (ankles). The celebration lasts no more than two hours and thirty minutes, allowing everyone ample time to change into their golf shoes and tee off by three o'clock.

IV. THE OVERSTATED AFFAIR

A stunning vision of egomaniacal excess designed to outdo every wedding that has ever been or will ever be. The fripperies unfurl on a Caribbean island with a population far smaller than the number of spectators who will be flown in for this Happiest Week. Each day they'll delight in the minute-by-minute itinerary the couple has planned in their own honor, from pre-rehearsal hot-air-balloon black-tie breakfasts to semiformal dress-rehearsal scuba-and-softball dinner dances. When the big(gest) day arrives, a horse-drawn ticker tape parade leads the bride and groom to a solid gold Chinese pagoda they've had shipped over for the ceremony, fully updated with stadium-sized video projection screens allowing easy viewing for all. A flock of toucans shall be released following the exchange of vows, and then guests will be treated to dinner and dancing inside the "Tents of Many Nations." Once everyone has ogled over the loot displayed on a revolving conveyer belt in the Gift Tent while the New York Philharmonic plays "That's What Friends Are For," they'll convene in the Viennese Dessert Chalet and toast the couple until dawn.

Selecting a Service Provider

When searching for an officiant to conduct the wedding service, most Nearly-weds feel compelled to find someone who has had a powerful presence throughout their lives; someone both familiar and revered; someone they've known through childhood and adulthood. Unfortunately, the cast of "The Mary Tyler Moore Show" is not ordained to perform marriages, so they're forced to find a clergy person.

The most important trait to look for in a clergy person is that he or she is affiliated with a house of worship that will make a good backdrop for the photos in your wedding album. The second most important characteristic to look for is the person's ability to talk about you during the ceremony as though he or she has known you since childhood.

As for nonreligious or "heretic" Nearly-weds, there's a motley assortment of secular sermonizers to choose from, including: a ship's captain, a notary public, and a justice of the peace. When deciding which is right for you, ask yourselves some important questions, such as "Why are these people performing weddings rather than sailing a ship, notarizing, or doing whatever it is a justice of the peace is supposed to do?"

Clearly, the only qualified professional trained in matrimonial law is a judge. Start looking now to find one who can squeeze your wedding in between cases in divorce court.

Keeping the (Inter)faith

If the two of you are of different denominations and you'd like to avoid alienating either set of grandparents forever, why not have an interfaith ceremony? The challenge is convincing someone to conduct it, as rabbis, ministers, and other devout individuals don't like to share the pulpit with anyone. In religious circles, this is known as "holier than thou" behavior. To curtail it, compromise. Tell the minister you'll raise the children Christian, tell the rabbi you'll raise the children Jewish, and tell the grandparents you'll do whatever they want as long as they promise to baby-sit.

Theme Weddings: Experiments in Terror

In recent years, more couples have opted for special "theme weddings," an apparent reaction to that shopworn old theme of two people falling in love and spending their lives together. One fun-loving couple who met at a Star Trek convention, for instance, decided upon a "trekkie theme," in which the cake was fashioned to resemble the starship *Enterprise* and the attendants wore nutty, elongated ears such as those of Mr. Spock! Another couple shared a love for medieval history and had a "Renaissance wedding" that gave their guests a rare opportunity to dress in period costumes, test their hand at jousting, and feast upon roasted pheasant—using only their fingers! Yes, theme weddings are as varied and unique as the diseased minds that think them up and inflict them on others. If you prefer a more universal theme, choose one of the old chestnuts below:

THE SHOTGUN WEDDING

A popular theme for all you Nearly-weds who can't wait to settle down and start a family. Twenty-four hours after the test strip turns blue, invitations are E-mailed, a wedding gown[8] is delivered from the Big, Beautiful Women catalog, and a groom is identified through a series of DNA tests. Following the wedding, guests receive a combination thank-you note/birth announcement, and everyone pretends to believe the baby was "premature."

THE ETHNIC WEDDING

This theme helps you cash in on the ethnic background you forgot you had. To rediscover your Polish roots, the bride should wear a traditional "money dress," to which guests pin dollar bills in exhange for a dance. To celebrate your Chicano ancestry, incorporate a Mexican custom, such as the one requiring the best man[9] to pay for the rings. And to honor your Philippine lineage, remind the bride's

[8]off-white, empire waist
[9]*señor mas bien*

family to provide a generous cash dowry. By borrowing elements from each of your cultures, your wedding will be a richly rewarding experience.

THE SERIAL WEDDING

A favorite for those who liked getting married so much the first time, they want to do it again and again. Step one: Find a lifelong mate; marry mate; blame mate for ruining your life. Step two: Find a younger lifelong mate; marry mate; blame mate for ruining your life. Performed annually, the serial theme will keep any marriage feeling like puppy love.

THE SAME-SEX WEDDING

This all-inclusive theme features health insurance, tax breaks, and a fabulous honeymoon in Honolulu.

Where to Wed

....

Location Scouting

Traditionally, the bride picks a location that's best suited to *her* family, but I recommend picking a location best suited to *both* families, such as Micronesia. Don't worry if Micronesia seems like it's going to be an inconvenient wedding site for your families. That is the point. Besides, anywhere farther than the mall is going to be an inconvenient wedding site for your families, as they'll soon be letting you know through a series of colorful threats not to show up. Unfortunately, these threats usually ring hollow.

If you're having a modest wedding—i.e., one that doesn't entail renting out a mid-size Polynesian island chain—you may want to save Micronesia for the honeymoon and conduct the wedding . . .

In a Church or Temple!

If you are churchgoing Nearly-weds, spending your Happiest Day with an individual fastened to a crucifix will remind you who you truly are in this wayward world: a couple of godless heathens who've been living in sin and are going straight to hell immediately following the garter toss.

As for the synagogue-style setting, it provides a place to engage in ancient, ethnic wedding traditions such as whipping your guests into a group vegetative coma by reciting ceaseless Hebrew passages that translate into English as: "We're a couple of godless heathens who've been living in sin and are going straight to hell immediately following the hora." Which is why you might opt to hold the entire wedding . . .

At Home!

To add that personal touch, many wedding books suggest making an entrance down the marble staircase of your home and holding the ceremony by the fireplace. Before you feel inadequate, remember: The authors of these books have never visited a Nearly-wed home. If they had, they'd know the staircase usually leads to the scary coughing lady's apartment in the attic, and the closest thing to a fireplace is a space heater that causes a city-wide blackout any time it is used.

In this case, the experts advise making your vows in the home where you grew up. This is excellent advice as long as you overlook the fact that (a) the strangers who are now living in the home where you grew up are reserving it for *their* children's weddings, and (b) the last vow you remember making in this home was the one to run away from it. Besides, getting married in your parents' home only reinforces their already staunch misunderstanding that this is *their* wedding, not yours. But don't despair! Finding neutral turf is as easy as tying the knot . . .

In a Function Hall!

Sooner or later, you may want to believe that a climate-controlled compound designed in Early Department of Motor Vehicles decor will make your guests feel right at home. After all, you'll reason, they've already been to thirty other weddings there this month alone! They already know where to stand for a view of the ceremony that's less blocked by the steel beams disguised as palm trees!

As you continue struggling to look on the bright side, you'll stop thinking of the function hall as a cold and impersonal wedding space. You'll start thinking of ways to make it *your* cold and impersonal wedding space. Perhaps you can fashion your own unique corsages out of festive "Hello

My Name Is" tags to distinguish your guests from the members of the Policemen's Benevolent Association who'll be meeting on the other side of the divider wall. And for centerpieces, how about some brightly colored oxygen tanks, bursting with lilies and daffodils, to ensure continued breathing once the air supply has been completely depleted from the building. On the other hand, you can always cut costs by conducting your Happiest Day . . .

In a Tent!

For an outdoor affair, this is a dream—until it becomes that classic Nearly-wed nightmare in which flash floods come gushing through the roof, gale-force winds send cutlery crashing through the air, and a raging cyclone hoists the Big Top off the ground and hurls your guests to Kingdom Come. When you wake up, splash some cold water on your face and book the next flight to . . .

Las Vegas!

An ideal choice if you're a fun-loving Nearly-wed who's reviewed all the options and decided you'd rather be shooting craps and drinking Bahama Mamas in the Woo-Woo Lounge than searching for a wedding site.

Brochures and Other Great Works of Fiction

Once you've determined a general setting in which to wed, the next step is identifying some specific reception sites, which you should do whenever you get back from Las Vegas. Most Nearly-weds begin by ordering a directory such as "Fantabulous Weddings at Splendiferous Places," available through your local chamber of commerce or Better Business Bureau department of consumer fraud. If, for some reason, the guide arrives before your wedding date, share some quality time admiring the expertly retouched photos and imaginative descriptions:

Shangri-la De Da:
Special Day *Specialists!*

Set on 253,000 acres of tropical New England farmland, manicured white sand dunes, and flowering Redwood jungles that rise majestically from our award-winning sea, this cozy medieval castle features spectacular views of Mount Kilimanjaro, and is surrounded by its very own full-spectrum rainbow, promising a genuine pot of twenty-four-karat gold for each couple lucky enough to wed beneath its historic, life-giving gazebo. Available for conferences.

When to Wed

....

Setting the Date

This is as simple as deciding upon your favorite time of year, and calling reception sites to discuss availability.

MANAGER: Hello when will you be getting married with us please?

YOU: We are thinking of getting married in June.

MANAGER (wistfully): Ah . . . June. Of what year?

YOU: Uh . . . this year?

MANAGER (choking on petit four): Good one! But seriously, we have an opening on the Tuesday morning of the dawning of the second ice age. Will that be cash or charge?

Resetting the Date

This task is marked by the frenzied phoning of any establishment listed under *W* in the Yellow Pages. To save time and long-distance costs, don't do this at home by yourself. Do it at the office with everyone else who is pretending to be working while they are really planning their weddings. For maximum workplace productivity, delegate duties. Hire a few interns to make a database of all dwellings in the greater tri-nation area that will be vacant sometime in June. Tell your assistants they'll be downsized unless they produce a site-acquisition plan before the designated deadline for marriage. Launch an incentive program to motivate the telemarketing staff.

Once you collect a list of venues that are still available,[10] call them yourself to compare prices. This is your chance to judge whether it's worth taking time to see each place in person. Don't shilly-shally around:

MANAGER: Hello when will you be getting married with us please?

YOU: Not so fast, pal. First tell me how much you charge.

MANAGER: We have a lovely wraparound verandah that seats sixty-five thousand, and a glass-enclosed atrium that is perfect for a sunset cocktail hour.

YOU: Great, let's talk bottom line.

MANAGER: I almost forgot to tell you about the Surrey

[10]Example: "Big Al's Meat Locker"

Room! It seats three, making it ideal for an intimate gathering; I *know* you would love it.

YOU: How much is it?

MANAGER: Yes, splendid views indeed.

Seeing Is Unbelieving

....

Venue Visitation Advice

When making appointments to see potential wedding spots, never restrict yourself to sites that sound promising. Sites that sound promising are wildly out of your price range. Sites that don't sound promising are also wildly out of your price range. Thus you need to visit each and every site that is wildly out of your price range.

The best time to visit such a site is on the same morning of the same day of the same week you are supposed to be visiting all the other sites that are wildly out of your price range. Why? Because that is the only time the manager can fit you in.

For a sneak preview, let's catch up with our fictional case-study Nearly-weds, "Stan" and "Peg," who—as previously noted—are in no way based upon me, Dan, and my lovely, nonfictional bride, Meg.

In Search of a Wedding Site:
A Day in the Life of "Stan" and "Peg"

4:00 A.M. Green Field Gardens

It is a raw, dreary daybreak when they pull up to Green Field Gardens, and before they've even turned off the windshield wipers, Stan and Peg are accosted by the Greenfields, an elderly couple sporting matching pastel baseball caps and gardening mitts. "You two are adorable!" gushes Mrs. Greenfield. "Now, quick like a bunny, let's take a stroll out in our field!"

Trudging through a muddy patch of crabgrass, it soon becomes evident that the "field" is a softball field. "You've got to imagine it in June," says Mr. Greenfield, "with all those little yellow flowers—what are they called again, Mother?" "Dandelions," Mrs. Greenfield shouts. "Yes! Dandy-lions!" echoes Mr. Greenfield, who leads the way to a rusted batting cage speckled with pigeon excrement. "Now, *this*, my darlings," Mrs. Greenfield boasts, "*THIS* is our gazebo. You've got to imagine it in June, when we paint it white and tie a balloon to it. Ready to walk down the aisle?" Dodging the poison ivy, the four of them parade arm in arm from home plate to the pitcher's mound, where the ceremony is to be conducted. "We'll get rid of these garbage cans in June," Stan and Peg are assured.

And as they round third base for the dugout ("bride's dressing room"), they finally break free of the Greenfields' grasp and gauge each other's opinions of the site. It is a refrain that will become familiar in the course of the day . . .

STAN: I know it sounds crazy, but . . . I love it!
PEG: I hate it.

5:00 A.M. Bonbon Manor

The foyer features gilded cathedral ceilings and Italian mosaic floors. The banquet hall is graced by Persian rugs and crystal chandeliers. Signed Monets line the parlor walls. "And now, my dear friends Stanley and Peggetha, allow me to escort you into the West Wing," offers the guide, a gentleman in a satin smoking jacket who has identified himself as "the baron." The West Wing is a mildew-ridden screened-in porch with indoor/outdoor carpeting and a Ping-Pong table in the corner.

"The West Wing is where we conduct our weddings," the baron proclaims in his unidentifiable foreign accent. "You really *must* try to imagine it in June." Stan and Peg try to imagine it in June. They imagine a mildew-ridden screened-in porch with indoor/outdoor carpeting and a Ping-Pong table in the corner. And ants. The baron gazes upon them with his twitching glass eye, as if he knows precisely what each of them is thinking . . .

STAN: Okay, we'll take it!
PEG: I hate it.

6:00 A.M. Whispering Corks Vineyard
STAN: Love it!
PEG: Hate it.

7:00 A.M. Lillywhite Country Club
STAN: Love it!
PEG: Hate it.

8:00 A.M. Interstate 95 Rest Stop
STAN: Love it!
PEG: This is a rest stop, not a wedding place, you bonehead.

9:00 A.M. Hotel Sofisticato
After drag-racing through several time zones in their desperate search for a space, Stan and Peg have landed at the tiniest hotel in town, where they're being ushered about by a small, excitable woman wearing large, jangling bracelets. "I feel very close to you two already," confides Bracelets, who has informed them several times that she is the hotel's "senior hospitality coordinator." "As *senior hospitality coordinator*, here is what I thought the second the doorman let you in: 'The Wainwrights. Now, *there* is a couple with true sophistication.'" Though Stan is exhausted, he musters the courtesy of a reply. "We are the Lutzes," he says.

Unfazed, Bracelets grabs her silver-plated clipboard and jangles them forth: The Main Ballroom ("Do you two know the Rockefellers? Cookie and Sumner were married here last spring!"); The Penthouse Dining Club ("Didn't I see you both here last night for Henrick the Crown Prince of Iceland's wedding?"); The Kitty Carlisle Hart Memorial Coat Check Hall ("You *must* imagine this area in June, when all the extinct animal furs are replaced by lightweight Armani wraps spun by authentic Turkish silkworms.")

By the time they're done, Stan and Peg's heads are spinning, and all the places they've seen today begin melding into one nameless, shapeless blur. Bracelets' earsplitting voice jolts them back to reality. "Kids, you get married with us and you won't have to worry about anything!" she shrieks. "We're a hotel! We do EVERYTHING." This gets them thinking . . .

STAN: I hate it.
PEG: I love it.

June 1 Hotel Sofisticato
STAN: I do.
PEG: I do.

Uncovering Hidden Costs

In their giddy excitement to secure that perfect site, many Nearly-weds wind up clearing out their life savings. I don't recommend this approach, since it leaves no money left over to cover "hidden" costs, such as taxes, overtime fees, and the cardiac resuscitation equipment you'll require once the *real* bill arrives. To prevent small surprises before it's too late, fill out the following worksheet for each site you consider.

Handy Hidden Cost Worksheet

INCLUDED IN COST	HIDDEN COST	TOTAL
The facility	cover charge to enter facility	$_____,000,000,000,000,000
	departure tax to exit facility	$_____,000,000,000,000,000
	facility fumigation fee	$_____,000,000,000,000,000
Tablecloths	tables	$_____,000,000,000,000,000
Gratuities for wait and kitchen staff	wait staff	$_____,000,000,000,000,000
	kitchen staff	$_____,000,000,000,000,000
Champagne toast	"corking fee"	$_____,000,000,000,000,000
	chilling fee	$_____,000,000,000,000,000
	pouring fee	$_____,000,000,000,000,000
	clinking of glasses for toast fee	$_____,000,000,000,000,000
	swallowing fee	$_____,000,000,000,000,000
		$_____,000,000,000,000,000

Making the Cut

....

Who to Invite

When you first sit down to plan your guest list, you'll want to invite approximately everyone you've ever met in your entire lives. This often proves impractical. After all, your parents have already invited everyone they've ever met in *their* entire lives.[11] What's a Nearly-wed to do? Simply split the guest list into equivalent parts: one third for the groom's parents, one third for the bride's, and another third for the two of you. Let's say you want a total of 150 guests. Once everyone has compiled their lists, expect the numbers to look something like this:

- Groom's parents: 350 people
- Bride's parents: 672 people
- Remaining space for Nearly-weds: *-872 people*

[11]and their next of kin

Once you point out this disparity to your parents, expect their responses to sound something like this:

- "Don't worry, most of the people on our list won't come."
- "Then again, maybe they will. Who knows? We haven't talked to them in thirty years."
- "The rest of our list is in the mail."

How to Limit Your List

Begin by giving some thought to the one most important person you absolutely want to be there. If you're like most Nearly-weds, your thoughts will flow along the following lines . . .

Best friend *OONA* from high school.
If I invite Oona from high school, I have to invite **INA** *from high school. If I invite Ina from high school, I have to invite* **SONNY** *from junior high. If I invite Sonny from junior high, I have to invite* **EVERYONE FROM JUNIOR HIGH.** *If I invite everyone from junior high, I have to invite* **EVERYONE FROM GRAMMAR SCHOOL.** *If I invite everyone from* **MY** *grammar school, I have to invite* **EVERYONE FROM EVERY GRAMMAR SCHOOL.** *If I invite everyone from every grammar school in* **MY** *district, I have to invite* **EVERYONE FROM EVERY GRAMMAR SCHOOL IN EVERY DISTRICT IN EVERY COUNTRY.**
Preliminary guest list: 4.3 quadzillion

Cutting Your List

The goal here is to make yourself feel less like a monster as you alienate friends and family by slashing them off your guest list. Maintaining your dignity is as easy as coming up with a justification for expunging each victim.

Right now, review all the people on your list and think of one reason not to invite them. It doesn't have to be that they *did* something to you. Perhaps they're just not photogenic enough, or maybe you never really liked them in the first place, but just didn't know how to get the message across. Let's start with your best friend Oona from high school. Remember that time Oona borrowed your Wite-Out and returned it without the cap? Put a big red slash through Oona's name *right now*. See how exhilarating this is! Simply by axing your best friend, you've single-handedly annihilated 4.3 quadzillion other guests. Now use the following classification system to determine who *really* deserves an invitation:

THE A LIST

- All your relatives who live too far away to come, but will still send a good gift
- All your parents' friends who live too far away to come but will still send a good gift
- All your friends

THE B LIST

- Emergency guests you E-mail at the last minute to fill in for no-shows with "car trouble"[12]
- People you were close to ten years ago but aren't close to now.
- People you're close to now but probably won't be in ten years
- People you invite to the ceremony but not the reception
- Guilt Guests you invite strictly because they invited you to theirs

THE BLACKLIST

- Insignificant Others
- Male children who are not bearing rings
- Female children who are not holding flowers
- Anyone from work who is not in a position to promote you
- All your ex-girlfriends/boyfriends who are more attractive than you've let on to your fiancé[13]
- Anyone you owe more than fifteen dollars
- Anyone who didn't get you anything last time you got married
- Everyone who believed you when you claimed, *"This wedding is going to be really small."*

[12]Note: Last-minute emergency guests will always be the hit of the wedding
[13]Especially: ex-girlfriends of the bride; ex-boyfriends of the groom

Cutting Your Fiancé's List

Once you've cut all the people off your guest list, the next thing you have to do is: cut more people off your guest list. How about cutting your fiancé? He or she will be around for the rest of your life. Is it going to kill you if you're not together on one lousy day?

If this idea sounds good to you, you appear to be on the brink of a Nearly-wed nervous breakdown. Perhaps it's time you paused to regain your perspective. Your fiancé is your soul mate. Your fiancé makes you feel special; beautiful; needed. How crazy you were only one paragraph ago to even *consider* cutting your fiancé from your guest list!

If your fiancé insists on attending the wedding, it's only fair that all remaining cuts should come from your fiancé's list. Try your best to be diplomatic, just like fictional case-study Nearly-weds Stan and Peg, who are in no way based upon me, Dan, or my lovely, nonfictional bride, Meg.

PEG: Um, honey? I noticed you put Eugene Lutz on your list. Do you really think he has to be there?

STAN: Well, he *is* my brother . . .

PEG: That's not the point!

STAN: What *is* the point?

PEG: The point is, we have to knock one more person off this list to make sure there's a meal for the drummer!

To Pad or Not to Pad? (Not to Pad)

Since it's estimated that 10 percent of those invited won't show up, nervous Nearly-weds often pad their list with auxiliary guests to compensate. What they don't realize is that the 90 percent who do show up will be padding the list *for* them, graciously supplying surplus dates, offspring, baby-sitters, hitchhikers, etc. As we see, padding the guest list is one task that will thankfully take care of itself, leaving you free to concentrate on more pressing matters, like hiring a bouncer to work the door.

Guest-o-Nomics

In the ruthless game of guest-list negotiations, it all comes down to the bottom line: Who is worth the price you're paying per plate and who isn't? Before investing in anyone, I advise conducting a rigorous cost/benefit analysis to determine the value of adding him or her to your portfolio (see opposite). Don't fret over those "junk guests" you're forced to liquidate. Instead, invite them all to an "engagement party" where you can cut your losses and recoup their gifts.

Guest Cost/Benefit Analysis

GUEST OPTION	RISK FACTOR	PROFIT POTENTIAL	GUEST RATING INDEX (GRI)
• Grandpa Ralphy	• likelihood he'll expose himself to bridesmaids	• 1 itchy afghan obtained free with checking account	• CUT
• Dr. & Mrs. Bernie Rabinowitz	• never go anywhere without pet Chihuahuas "Coco" and "Kissy"	• $250 check	• A LIST
• Cousin Jenny's blowhard husband, Hiram	• will never again speak to our parents if not invited	• will never again speak to *us* if not invited	• B LIST

Anointing the Attendants

....

Why You Should Pick a Wedding Party

Selecting a wedding party is a wonderful tradition because it obligates people to throw you a shower or bachelor party. The first slots to fill on your staff are maid of honor and best man. The maid of honor should be a sister or friend who can give the bride the emotional support she'll need to get through the ceremony, such as prescription-strength antianxiety medication, tranquilizer darts, or simply a standard-issue stun gun. As for the best man, grooms can use this helpful scale to rank all contestants:

A Best Man is Hard to Find

GOOD	BETTER	BEST
• older brother	• younger brother	• Allman brother
• introduced you to first girlfriend	• introduced you to fiancée	• introduced you to Pamela Lee Anderson
• would never tell anyone about your relationship with the cafeteria lady from college	• would never tell anyone about your relationship with "Dominatrica" from the "Spank Me, Auntie!" chat room	• would never tell anyone about the cafeteria lady and Dominatrica during his toast at your wedding

Bridesmaid Psychology

When faced with the delicate task of designating brides-maids, the female Nearly-wed must weigh the following emotional factors:

1. Some women are going to be annoyed if you don't choose them.[14]

[14]particularly those you haven't talked to since Brownies

2. The rest of the women are going to be annoyed if you do choose them.

I know what you're thinking: Hold on! How could anyone possibly be annoyed if I grant them a bridesmaid's appointment?! Consider the following possibilities: They'll be annoyed because (a) they've been bridesmaids in approximately thirteen billion other weddings this year and have already applied for state aid just to pay for the color-coordinated two-tone opalescent canary yellow triple-strap, single-buckle, flat-heeled, open-toed Versace sandals you've "suggested" they wear, and they'll be annoyed because (b) you didn't pick them for maid of honor.

As we see, the best idea is to select only bridesmaids you want to annoy. In keeping with tradition, dress them in mermaid-style floral prom gowns that make them look like grotesque sea monsters, while you look like a stunning supermodel goddess.

Groomsmen at-a-Glance

Groomsmen are chosen on the basis of whoever is left standing after the bachelor party.

Proper Attendant Abuse

In your crankiest moments, you may be tempted to act as if the role of the attendants is to *attend* to your every need. Yet it would be selfish to sit back as they wait on you hand and foot. Instead, help them out by providing a list of duties they'll be expected to perform in exchange for the commemorative pen-and-pencil party favors you'll reward them with upon emancipation. Here's a guide to get them started:

The Attendant's Checklist

○ Help Nearly-weds shop for wedding clothes.
○ Help Nearly-weds shop for groceries.
○ Pay for Nearly-weds' groceries.
○ Pay for Nearly-weds' honeymoon.
○ Pay Nearly-weds' rent.
○ Clean Nearly-weds' bathtub.
○ Fix Nearly-weds' VCR.
○ Tolerate Nearly-weds' tantrums.
○ Take Nearly-weds' abuse.
○ Act like you're having fun.

Nearly-wed
Nitty-Gritty

Face the Music

....

Mood Music: Less Is Too Much

As you zero in on all the details that go into planning the perfect party, remember: The phrase "Music sets the mood" does *not* mean your wedding will be a flop unless every moment is scored like the soundtrack to a Merchant-Ivory production. Still, don't be surprised if you find the following thoughts racing through your mind the next time you're pretending to pay attention at an important business meeting:

"Okay, we'll need a classical harp ensemble playing *The Pachelbel Canon in D Major* when the guests first arrive, a strolling minstrel violinist to accompany us down the aisle, a blaring crash of cymbals when we kiss, a New Orleans Dixie jazz band for the recessional, some light, jazzy glockenspiel while hors d'oeuvres are passed, a little Swiss yodeling during dinner—maybe a ukulele or flute-o-phone solo with salad, a barbershop quartet at dessert . . ."

Happily, all you *really* need to know about mood music

is: It's not going to affect anybody's mood. The only thing that's going to affect anybody's mood is: alcohol. Now, most of your guests are going to experience the peak mood-elevating properties of alcohol once the background music stops and the dancing begins. And by that time they'll be in such a good mood that they won't care *what* the music sounds like. This is very lucky, as anyone who has ever stayed sober and listened to a wedding band can tell you.

Battle of the Wedding Bands

Nearly-weds who prefer live[15] musicians at their reception have two choices: a "specialty" band, which plays *one* type of music badly; or a "versatile" band, which plays *many* types of music badly. To be safe, stick with a versatile band. That way there will be something bad for everyone. You'll be able to spot a versatile band by the song list they give you:

SONG LIST FOR SISTAH YETTA MAMBAZO'MALLEY AND THE VERSATELLITES

1. "Hava Nagilah"
2. "Amazing Grace"
3. "Louie, Louie"

[15]or at least lifelike

How to Find the Band That's
Less Wrong for You

Crashing weddings of complete strangers is a proven technique for discovering new talent. If you're uncomfortable attending parties you were not invited to, I suggest inviting friends and family to go with you. This way you'll have more people to judge the band's ability to play "It's My Party," "Hail, Hail, the Gang's All Here," and all the other songs you request. You'll also have more people to judge the food, wine, party favors, best man's toast, bridesmaids' figures, etc. By the time you're all escorted out,[16] you'll know what to ask for at the next wedding to which none of you is invited.

The Beauty of Booking Agents

The advantage of agents is that they'll give you information on all the acts they represent, so you can systematically eliminate each one of them from your search. Here's how: Let's say you tell Agent X you want a rhythm and blues band for your reception on Saturday night, June 1. In turn, Agent X will send you a fourteenth-generation dubbed tape of a mariachi band that is available on Tuesday morning, March 8. Along with the tape, Agent X will add an amusing

[16]by the police

eight-by-ten glossy of the band posing as real musicians in their sequined matador-style tuxedos. He or she will also add several forged letters of recommendation:

```
        To whom it may concern:
I highly recommend the Musical Muchachos.
             Love,
         Queen Elizabeth
```

The last thing the agent will add is an extra 10 to 110 percent commission to the cost of hiring any band. This should help clinch your decision not only to eliminate the band, but to eliminate the middleman as well.

Wooing the Talent

When courting wedding musicians directly, don't be misled by the cliché that they're all second-rate, talent-free hacks. Most of them are fourth-rate, talent-free hacks who are under the impression that they are legendary supergroups. If you ever expect to sign one of them for your Happiest Day, you must indulge their delusions of grandeur.

YOU: I have been a huge fan of yours for years, Maestro. Tell me about some of your latest projects.
GUS DELVECHIO, OF THE GUS DELVECHIO SEXTET: I am shocked by your ignorance of our work. In addition to

playing the McDermott wedding, for which we are best known, we have also performed at the marriage of Babette and Hank Einhorn, for which we were inducted into the Wedding Musicians Hall of Fame. We have a huge following in Japan, where we recently picked up a Japanese Grammy award for our triple-platinum album, *Live at the Fujisaka-Hoshirama Wedding.*

YOU: Mr. Maestro, you are truly a musical luminary. I'd be honored to book you for my wedding reception.

GUS DELVECHIO: Please. We are not the kind of band that has to play *weddings.*

Important Interview Questions for the Wedding Band

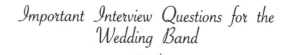

1. Don't you think taking eighteen breaks is a little excessive?
2. Do you find it fashionable to perform in shimmering lime green tuxedos?
3. Do you promise not to play "Once, Twice, Three Times a Lady?"
4. Do you know how to play our special song?
5. "Once, Twice, Three Times a Lady" is not our special song.
6. Do you prefer pasta or a cold-cut plate for dinner?
7. Oh, really? And how do you like your prime rib done?

Getting Down With the DJ

If you're looking for a cheap alternative to a live band and are unfamiliar with the phrase "You get what you pay for," hire a disc jockey. A disc jockey is an individual who acts out his unsavory fantasies of being Peter Frampton, Rock God, by coming to your wedding in a tight tuxedo T-shirt and sunglasses, and air-guitaring along with all the classic hits he masturbated to as a teenager. Some DJs are former AVs, or members of the audiovisual squad in high school. Remember that nine-foot-tall kid Norman Mellman, who used to set up the loudspeakers for the school band concerts? Norman is now "Dee-J Doctor Normy-Norm Spinmaster MC." Other DJs are former JDs, or juvenile delinquents. How do you think they amassed such a huge CD collection and those high-tech headphones?

Does Your DJ Have What it Takes?

DJs are available in a wide assortment of personalities. Before purchasing one, ask yourself: Do I want a DJ who is . . .

    a. outgoing and zany ___
    b. plucky and lovable ___
    c. gagged and muzzled ___

If you checked *c,* you are right! The personality trait of being "gagged and muzzled" will prevent your DJ from opening his mouth, ensuring a good time for all. Otherwise, he'll be inclined to emcee your reception with the gusto of a game-show host:

"Ladies and germs, may I direct your attention to the top of Staircase Number Four, where our lovely bride and groom are about to make their entrance! Come on down, Betty and Jerome! Ooops, sorry. Come on down, Peg and Stan! And now, may I direct your attention to the back of the room where Bridesmaid Number Two is coming out of the little girls' room with the groom's father! Well, she's a hot little ticket, ain't she, folks? How about a round of applause for that pair of gams! Coming up next, my sizzling laser light show. But now, without further ado, let's take a listen to the extended remix version of "Ooh Baby, I Love Your Way" from *Frampton Comes Alive!* Woo-eee! Let's get this party started!"

Important Questions for the DJ

1. Would you mind trying on this muzzle?

Catering. To Everyone.

....

The Key to a Perfect Meal

There are many important questions to ask yourselves regarding the cuisine for your reception, the most urgent of which is: open bar or cash bar?

Once you've done some hands-on research, move on to more detailed culinary concerns, such as whether to keep your open bar open for the entire reception, the first hour only, or alternating fourteen-minute shifts until the second champagne toast; whether to serve real champagne or sparkling wine; whether to serve "premium" or "house" sparkling wine; and whether it's not such a bad idea after all to inscribe BYOB underneath RSVP on your wedding invitations. You may also want to consider serving some food.

An Introduction to Wedding Food

Before you can even consider choosing the food, you must understand the subtle value judgments that emerge when civilian food crosses over into the realm of wedding food. Let us consider our old friend the chicken. In the civilian world, the venerable, versatile chicken is perhaps the only food everyone can agree upon. In fact, some of us enjoy a tasty, delicious chicken dish almost every day. Yes, we all love the chicken.

In the rarefied world of wedding cuisine, however, we learn that Mr. Chicken is to be treated as a second-class citizen. We find ourselves feeling that our former friend the chicken is cheap, and wrong. "If we serve chicken," we fear, "we will bring immeasurable shame upon ourselves and our families."

What accounts for these strange, shifting perceptions of poultry prestige? The same thing that accounts for those strange, shifting perceptions of everything else concerning your wedding: the lingering fear that your guests are going to pass judgment on it[17] behind your back. To prevent that fear from becoming a reality, you must reconcile *your* ideas about the wedding food with your *guests'* ideas about the wedding food.

[17]and you

Your Ideas About the Wedding Food

"We are spending a lot of money to feed these people. They'll be grateful no matter what we serve them."

Your Guests' Ideas About the Wedding Food

"We are spending a lot of money to buy these people a gift. They better have prime rib."

Are You Through with Your Prime Rib, Madame?

As we learn from the preceding comparative data, certain guests will pass judgment on your wedding unless you serve prime rib. This doesn't mean they're going to *eat* the prime rib, however. They're going to be far too full after deliberately consuming their body weights in hors d'oeuvres. Why? Because they're savvy enough to know that the prime rib— in the culinary tradition of wedding entrées since the marriage of Adam and Eve—is going to taste like shower curtains. Here is a typical discussion:

GUEST I (*shoveling a cheese platter down his throat*): So how was the Mermin wedding last week?

GUEST II (*chugging down a punch bowl of shrimp cocktail sauce*): Chintzy, chintzy, chintzy. They served chicken instead of prime rib. *Burp.*

Menu Mania

If your reception site doesn't dispense foodstuffs, you'll be forced to call a bunch of independent caterers and ask them to send sample menus, to which they will reply: "Do you honestly think we have time to send sample menus? We are *very* much in demand." Immediately upon hanging up, they will bombard you with enough sample menus to fill a recycling bin, somehow finding time in their demanding schedules to harass your answering machine with desperate follow-up calls such as: "Just a reminder that we are still *very* much in demand. We'll E-mail more menus and call back again in five minutes."

Once you've installed extra RAM to read all of these menus, start comparing prices. But remember: The difference between paying $10 per person and $110 per person has nothing to do with the food. It has everything to do with the presentation.

Price: $10 per person
Menu: Prime rib, mashed potatoes

Price: $110 per person
Menu: An eclectic mélange of prime fire-roasted Colorado free-range medallions of steer au jus, lovingly hand-carved and served piping hot with a seasonal presentation of individually peeled and mashed *pommes coulées tapanade brandade dacquoise aioli.*

The Joy of Tasting

Once you've perused your quadzillionth menu, the next step is visiting potential caterers for "a tasting," more commonly known as "a free lunch." Oddly, many Nearly-weds are intimidated by this singularly beautiful concept, worried that they don't know enough about food to critique it.

For this reason, I suggest limiting your tastings to caterers who also let you taste the wine. This will help both of you feel less self-conscious when you find yourselves saying things like: "Oh yes, we agree *entirely* that this exquisite little Vin Santo is the perfect dessert wine to complement your signature rolled fondant wedding cake. In fact, it's probably our favorite of *all* the dessert wines we enjoy each evening with our fondant, isn't it, honey? I said, ISN'T IT, honey? Oh, yes indeed. Can I have another canapé?"

Of course, the best reason to go on tastings is that they're the only chance you're going to get to taste your wedding food. Once the big day rolls around, you're going to be far too nervous/distracted/busy/hysterical/elated/medicated/delirious/confused to taste *anything*. So go with gusto to as many tastings as you possibly can. And when you finally find something that will appeal to *everyone* —your vegetarian guests, your kosher guests, your macrobiotic, microbiotic, and antibiotic guests —then and only then should you think about . . .

Sharing the Menu with Mom

Author's Note: *The fictional dialogue below is in no way based upon any conversation that ever transpired between my nonfictional bride, Meg, and her lovely mother. Especially that conversation they had about the menu.*

PEG: Hey, Mom! We've finally planned the perfect menu! Take a look and tell us what you think!

MOM (glancing at menu for .2 nanoseconds): I've got two words for you.

PEG: Yeah?

MOM: Lulu Vandermeyer.

PEG: Who's Lulu Vandermeyer?

MOM: Who's Lulu Vandermeyer? She's only the lady who lived next door to us for a month when you were five weeks old and has been looking forward to your wedding for the past twenty-seven years, that's who.

PEG: What does Lulu Vandermeyer have to do with our menu?

MOM: Two words.

PEG: Yeah?

MOM: Lactose-intolerant.

Flower Power Plays

....

Petal Pushing

Of all the details that make planning a wedding such a joy, most Nearly-weds have the strongest opinion on the subject of flowers.

The Bride's Opinion on the Subject of Flowers: "I refuse to spend a skillion dollars on the flowers."

The Groom's Opinion on the Subject of Flowers: "Not only do I refuse to spend a skillion dollars on the flowers, I refuse to spend a single cent on the flowers. None of the guests are going to remember the flowers. I want nothing to do with the flowers. I resent those flowers! I beg of you, *stop talking about the flowers!* Please pass the remote control."

How ironic, then, that the two of you are about to become an amateur horticultural team. You're going to recognize the difference between alstroemerias, stephanotis, and button chrysanthemums. You're going to develop deep-seated beliefs that orchids work only in large spaces with high ceilings, and scarlet gladioli have no place at an afternoon affair. You're going to know that zinnias symbolize lasting affection, cut-leaved coneflowers are mildly toxic to livestock, and wartberry fairybells are indigenous to eastern North Dakota.

And to whom are you going to owe all this newfound respect for the wonders of botany? Why, the same person to whom you are also going to owe two skillion dollars in cash or certified money order: that petal-pushing prima donna with the green thumb and the artistic temperament known as . . .

The Floriste

In all likelihood, your *floriste* will be known as Yasmine or Guillermo,[18] and will be either a fashionably earthy woman who favors chenille prairie skirts, or an impeccably groomed gentleman who also favors chenille prairie skirts. If he or she is an experienced *floriste*, Yasmine or Guillermo will have "florally orchestrated" the wedding space at thousands of events before yours, so (a) they are going to do the exact same thing they have always done, regardless of your personal taste in flowers, or (b) they are going to do

---

[18] Real names: Jane; Guido

something radically new and experimental, regardless of your personal taste in flowers.

This will not stop them from scheduling a costly consultation so they can better pretend to care what your personal taste in flowers *is*. The fact that you do not have a personal taste in flowers makes this meeting even more surreal, as it did for our fictional case-study bride, "Peg" (who continues to be not at all based on my lovely, nonfictional bride, Meg):

GUILLERMO: Tell me, blossom, who are you deep down inside? You strike me as a peony person. Which genus of calla lily would you say best reflects your floral fantasy?

PEG: Um . . . I think we'd like to keep the flowers pretty simple. Maybe just some roses on each table.

GUILLERMO: I am sorry, but simple flowers are not available this time of year. What do you think of silverleaf Japanese palafoxia, dripping from the ceilings in great vines of spotted saxifrage and fringed grass of parnassias? Yes! I see an entire ecosystem! The floors, carpeted in velvety Spanish peat moss! The walls, alive with night-blooming tansy-leaved primrose! What color are the bridesmaids' dresses?

PEG: Blue. I think.

GUILLERMO: I am sorry, but blue flowers are not available this time of year. The bridesmaids will wear dusty peapod. And they'll hold identical daffodil nosegays tied together with hand-beaded French jacquard ribbon. How about *your* bouquet? Tell me, blossom, anything you want.

PEG: I was thinking of something small, I guess.

GUILLERMO: Small flowers are not available. You'll carry a field of long-stemmed sunflowers, three dozen birds of paradise, and a saguaro cactus gently rising from a cascade of one hundred thousand weeping willow branches. Groomsmen's lapels?

PEG: Groomsmen? I don't know . . . carnations?

GUILLERMO: NO CARNATIONS! *EVER!!!* I beg your pardon, I appear to have lost control there for a moment. Tell me, blossom, just how much money were you planning on spending for your floral fantasy?

PEG: Um, a hundred dollars?

GUILLERMO: Ha! What do you think, this stuff grows on trees?

A Field Guide to Wedding Flora

In the enchanted wedding woodlands, every available surface is camouflaged by flowers. Flowers in standing arrangements, altar arrangements, aisle arrangements. Flowers on the reception tables, on the cake table, on the cake. Flowers stitched into hair, pinned onto bosoms, and awarded to premium-level friends and family as if to say, "*You* are some*body*, for *you* have a flower."

How to identify the many varieties you'll need to pollinate your Happiest Day? Study the following field guide:

Wedding Flora:
Boquetias bridialous (bride's bouquet)

Distinguishing Characteristics:
This cumbersome flowering stump is believed to have stress-reducing properties for Nearly-wed females, providing support for shaking, trembling hands during the traditional migration down the aisle. Conversely, it is believed to have stress-*inducing* properties for *non*-Nearly-wed females, who must grapple the flora from its final airborne state.

Wedding Flora:
Groom's boutonniere (groom's boutonniere)

Distinguishing Characteristics:
none

Wedding Flora:
Corsagicus vexatious (corsage)

Distinguishing Characteristics:
A stubborn, weedlike growth which commonly clutches its tendrils into the bodice or wrist of mothers and grandmothers, respectively clashing with clothing and cutting off blood supply. Best cared for with antihistamine and scissors.

Wedding Flora:
Centerpiecious (centerpiece)

Distinguishing Characteristics:
These table-based buds appear in two varieties.

1. Centerpiecious minimus — the common, low-lying clusters emerging from the core of each guest table — are useful in stimulating deep conversation amongst strangers who have been randomly seated together, e.g., "These sure are nice flowers" and "Yes, they are."

2. Centerpiecious maximus—a towering jungle indigenous strictly to the head table. By obstructing all views, this dense brush offers Nearly-weds maximum mealtime coverage, preventing altercations with adjacent parents who are complaining that the music is too loud.

Botanist's note: Centerpiecious maximus has a particularly short life span, as it is typically chain-sawed down and stolen by guests who replant it at home to block the view of the neighbor's house.

A Picture Is Worth a Thousand Bucks

....

The Secret to Finding a Master Photographer

How many times have you found yourself flipping through another couple's wedding photos and thinking, "How is it that these two look a million times better in the pictures than they do in real life?" This is an inappropriate question. What you should really be thinking is, "I wonder if their photographer is available for *our* wedding."

Once you've secured this Master's name and number, pay him a visit to inspect his portfolio. Any misty-filter montages of couples with cupids floating overhead? Any still lifes of Fruit Cup with White Wedding Shoe poignantly shot through a keyhole? If not, listen excitedly as the Master recites The Wedding Photographer's Credo: "I'm not one of those pushy wedding photographers who gets into everyone's face. My style is to just fade into the background. I'm so unobtrusive, you won't even know I'm there."

Give the Master a deposit at once. Then just sit back and wait for him to arrive on your Happiest Day with a shaved head, Nazi insignia tattoos, and knee-high leather boots. He'll soon be winning everyone over with his unobtrusive demeanor: "Achtung! Table Four! Line up in order of descending height! Now, get down on your knees and climb into a pyramid formation in front of the ice sculpture! Grampa! Get that oxygen mask off your mouth and hoist the bride onto your shoulders! At my command, you shall all smile and say 'Muenster!' "

Arming Yourself with a Shot List

To make believe you have some control over your wedding photography, devise a list of the specific moments, individuals, and Byzantine stepfamily configurations you want shot.[19] Should you remember to give this list to your photographer, it could lessen the chances of receiving an eighteen-frame sequence of cousin Larry's uninvited date, Venus (in the red sequined tube top), but not a single shot of your oldest childhood chum who flew in on the red-eye from Helsinki.

Still, remember that your wedding photos—like your wedding—aren't only about you. The challenge of the shot

[19] A twenty-gauge sawed-off shotgun is recommended for particularly malevolent stepsiblings.

list is to combine the kind of shots both of *you* want with the kind of shots both of your *mothers* want.

Example of Shots You Want

Candid, spontaneous moments capturing the spirit of your wedding day.

Example of Shots Mothers Want

Staged, blow-by-blow chronicle of bride gussying up on wedding morning.

Final Shot List

- shot of bride brushing hair on wedding morning
- shot of bride's mother brushing bride's hair
- shot of maid of honor brushing bride's hair
- group shot: 150 wedding guests brushing bride's hair
- shot of bride screaming "stop brushing my hair!"
- shot of bride's mother crying
- shot of bride crying
- shot of bride screaming at photographer to get out
- shot of bride smashing camera lens with hairbrush
- groom (optional)

Helpful Photo Hints

1. Have all formal portraits taken prior to the ceremony. Though it is bad luck for the groom to see the bride before the ceremony, it is even worse luck for both parties to miss the cocktail hour after the ceremony.

2. Given the choice of having your photos slapped into an album by the photographer or creating a meaningful album for yourselves, always have your photos slapped into an album by the photographer. Once you are married, you'll never get around to putting your photos in an album for yourselves. You'll be too busy getting copies of them made for everyone else.

3. Resist the temptation to place disposable cameras on each table unless you are prepared to spend all your disposable income developing disposable pictures.

4. There is nothing funnier than looking at photos of people dancing.[20]

Scenes from a Wedding Video

It's always prudent to have the festivities videotaped for those who won't be able to see you get married. The reason they won't be able to see you get married is that you will be completely obscured by spotlights, boom

[20] except watching them on the video

mikes, and a twelve-foot-tall cameraman under the impression that your wedding is his ticket to the Sundance Film Festival.

But fear not if the pressures of show biz seem too great to handle on the Happiest Day of Your Life. With the videographer's help, you'll soon forget it is the Happiest Day of Your Life, and find yourself focusing completely on your on-camera performance:

SCENE: A chapel. The bride and groom gaze deeply into each other's eyes.

GROOM: With this ring I thee —

VIDEOGRAPHER: Cut! That's almost a wrap, folks, but let's try it one more time like you really mean it. Can we get rid of that old guy with the Bible? He's kind of obstructing my frame.

GROOM: Excuse me, but can someone please remind me what my motivation is?

BRIDE: You're not shooting me from profile, are you? My agent specifically added a clause in the contract stipulating that my best angle is straight on, head slightly tilted to the left. And when is that voice-over actress coming in to give my character her subtle British accent?

VIDEOGRAPHER: We're rollin', folks! Ring Exchange, Take Two! Work with me, people!

The Nearly-wed
Invitationals

....

Invitation Intimidation

All you need to know about invitations is that they come
in two types: The *Hoity-Toity* and the *Artsy-Fartsy*.

The Hoity-Toity, displayed in strange, bulging binders
wherever you buy birthday cards, is distinguished by (a)
Braille-style letters that someone decided are worth more
money than plain old flat letters, and (b) a bevy of envelopes.
At the very least, this bevy should include: a primary, outer-
shell envelope; a second-layer envelope within an envelope; a
smaller, self-addressed stamped envelope safeguarding a response card envelope; a waterproof, breathable envelope to
wick moisture away from each accompanying envelope; a
wind-resistant midlayer envelope; an inner/outer envelope
containing a general, all-purpose envelope; an air-mail envelope for a touch of worldliness; a heat-retaining, padded
envelope to protect the air-mail envelope; and a few random
"first-class mail" envelopes stuffed in for added prestige. It

is also customary to include a dainty little piece of tissue so recipients can wipe the sweat from their brow once they have excavated the invitation itself.

If you prefer a homespun invitation, go with the Artsy-Fartsy approach. For creative inspiration, visit some of those trendy, do-it-yourself stationers that specialize in paper with flowers squashed into it. There you'll find many like-minded Nearly-weds making invitations just like the one you had in mind, with one distinction: Theirs are better. This is nothing the artsy Nearly-wed can't rectify by spending more money.[21] Buy little satin ribbons and tie your envelopes up in a bundle. Stuff the envelopes with colorful peacock feathers and fourteen-karat gold glitter. Skip the dainty piece of tissue and spring for pastel-colored Kleenex with soothing aloe moisturizer.

Proper (Re)Wording of the Invitation

To give your guests the personalized attention they deserve, don't send the same invitation to everyone. Rather, review your A List, B List, and Blacklist, (see p. 66), and word each invitation accordingly:

---

[21] or stealing another couple's invitation

The pleasure of your company
is requested at the marriage of

Peg and Stan

Saturday, the fifteenth of June,
at 6 o'clock in the evening
Vermont Alpine Country Club

black tie optional

CHOICE OF ENTREE

prime rib __

salmon __

The A-List Map

*Absolutely no offense whatsoever
will be taken if you do not
attend the marriage of*

Peg and Stan

*Tuesday, the fifteenth of February,
at 6 o'clock in the morning
Vermont Alpine Country Club*

swimsuits optional

CHOICE OF ENTREE

egg salad ___
tofu products ___

The B-List Map

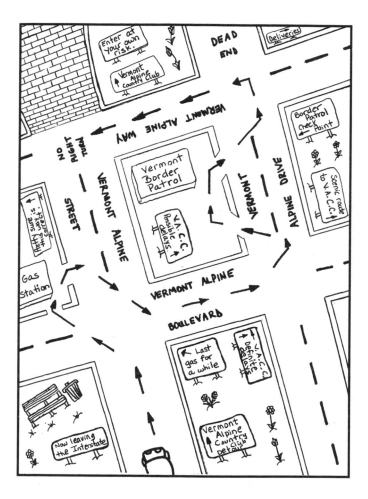

You have been intentionally excluded from attending the marriage of

Peg and Stan

at an undisclosed place and time that you will surely spend sitting in front of the TV in your underwear watching "BJ & the Bear" reruns on the USA Network like you do every day of your pathetic, miserable life while everyone else will be out sipping champagne and dancing under the stars to celebrate the Happiest Day of Our Lives, a day that will be even Happier because you won't be there and if you even try to crash, you will be arrested on site for vagrancy and thrown into the Big House.

CHOICE OF ENTREE

gruel ___

The Blacklist Map

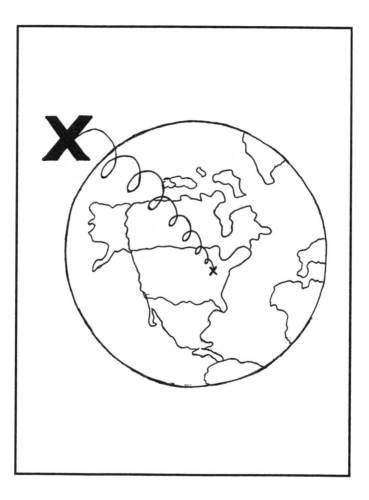

Adventures in Addressing

Because addressing envelopes is mind-bendingly tedious, don't waste time doing it yourself. That is what bridesmaids are for. Alternately, you can hire a calligrapher. A calligrapher's job is to reinterpret the alphabet into a language worth upwards of two dollars per envelope. If you are not fluent in this idiom, study the following . . .

English-to-Calligraphy Transcription Guide

ENGLISH
Captain and Mrs. Otto
Buttonweezer

CALLIGRAPHY

ellelele

RSVPs and Qs

When you send it out, a typical RSVP card looks something like this:

M_____will/will not attend.

When you get it back, a typical RSVP card looks something like these:

(A) The RSVP card from the people who try to be clever:

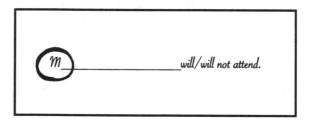

(B) The RSVP card from the people who are unclear on the concept of filling out the RSVP card:

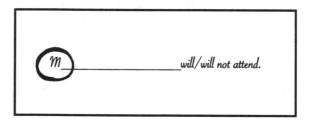

Of course, most of your close friends won't fall into either category, since most of your close friends won't RSVP. Some won't RSVP because they assume you know they're coming. Some won't RSVP because they assume you know they're coming and they're scared to tell you they're not. Some won't be counted among your close friends for very much longer at all.

Constructing Your Seating Plan:
Right This Way to Satan's Table!

The seating options for your reception are: Assigned Seats or General Admission. The Assigned Seats option is a highly structured strategy in which you spend six months painstakingly matching[22] the perfect meal-mates for each of your guests. The General Admission policy is what happens to the Assigned Seats plan once everyone has a cocktail, moves their chairs, and sits wherever the hell they please.

The trick to assigning seats is placing people together based on what they have in common. For example, Table 3 would be all the single people you're so subtly trying to fix up with future mates. Table 4 would be all the divorced people you're so subtly trying to separate from former mates. And Table 666 would be all the people who have in common that they have absolutely nothing in common.

In Nearly-wed mythology, Table 666 is known as Satan's Table. It is the final destiny of all those stray, oddball guests who haunt you relentlessly through the planning process, until your life becomes completely consumed with finding them a place to sit. Late one night, for instance, you'll be having passionate premarital sex, and in the heat of the moment, your partner[23] will start breathlessly moaning: "Mrs. Caruso! Mrs. Caruso!"

And all at once you'll roll over on your side, light a cigarette, and say, "I know. I was just thinking about her."

[22] and rematching
[23] preferably your fiancé

And your partner will whisper softly in your ear, "Do you want to try it again?"

And you will say, "Yes. Let's get out the seating chart and figure out where to put her once and for all."

The only way to pacify the dark gods of Satan's Table is to sacrifice yourself. Seat *yourselves* at Satan's Table, so everyone has the two of *you* in common.

Typical Satan's Table Seating
(consult diagram on following page)

1. Mrs. Caruso (late Grandma Belle's canasta partner)
2. Rain Krishna (bride's friend from night school decoupage class who doesn't know anyone else)
3. Mouthy Myrna Schultz (can talk to *anyone*)
4. Mute cousin Leon (can't talk to *anyone*)
5. Lars Ølafson (Danish exchange student living with groom's parents)
6. Identities Unknown (anonymous Nearly-wed couple crashing wedding to check out band)
7. Bride and groom (not based on author's bride and author)

Figure 666: Satan's Table (a.k.a. "head table")

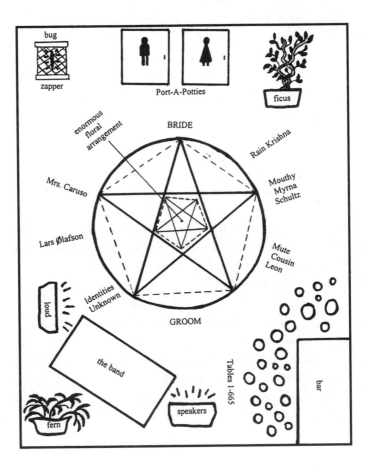

116 ∾ DAN ZEVIN

Dressed to Be Nearly-wed

....

A Wedding Gown Odyssey: "Peg's" Story

Author's note: *Despite the recent rage in cross-dressing, I myself have never actually shopped for nor tried on a wedding gown.*[24] *Therefore, to help all you Nearly-wed brides select your ceremonial garb, we are now going to follow the fictional case-study bride, "Peg," who is in no way based upon my lovely nonfictional bride, Meg. Really. I swear.*

Like most Nearly-wed brides, the first boutique Peg visits is the twenty-four-hour CVS, where she scans the literature on display next to the Chiclets, darts her eyes left and right to make sure no one is looking, and swiftly snatches up the bridal magazine (Headline: *Annual All-Ad Issue! Forty Thousand Dresses Starting At Forty Thousand Dollars!*) that she has been coveting since the day Luke and Laura got married on "General Hospital."

[24] Except that one time in college, but that was for a Zeta Psi Halloween party. Really. I swear.

The next morning, in the privacy of her padlocked office, Peg begins the traditional Nearly-wed custom of ripping apart this publication page by page until she finds a look she likes. It is an understated, elegant look, culled from the Carolyn Bessette Kennedy retrospective she finds on page 8,003. A "simple sheath," it is called in the caption. "Yes," thinks Peg, carefully placing a shot of Carolyn in her purse, "I shall wear a simple sheath."

Peg spends the following twenty-four hours forcing this photo on every female friend she has ever had. Each of them reacts the same way, fishing through their purses for the pages *they've* torn out of bridal magazines for Peg. Sheaths, all. Peg feels validated. Peg feels confident. Peg fells ready to share the selected sheath with her mother.

"Interesting," her mother remarks.

She knows what her mother means by "interesting." It means she finds the "suggestive" neckline completely inappropriate for Peg. It means she finds the "humdrum" design completely inappropriate for Peg. It means the only thing she finds remotely appropriate about the dress is the only thing that really *is* completely inappropriate for Peg: the color (white). Peg folds Carolyn up and puts her back in her purse. "So," she says, "we hired this guy Guillermo to do the flowers."

One afternoon on her lunch hour, Peg walks past a store called Madam Snootella's Bridal Boutique. She has passed this store every day for years, but only recently has she begun to notice it. It's as if her engagement ring is a radar, leading her to a matrimonial marketplace she was oblivious to before: The Invitation Station; Vera's Cakery Bakery; Tiffany's. She removes Carolyn from her purse before approaching Snootella's sleek glass doors. She rings the buzzer to get the attention of a platinum-haired woman seated behind the counter, smoking a long blue cigarette and flipping through *Town and Country*. She buzzes again. Finally the woman lifts her head and blows a stream of concentric smoke rings toward a sign by the door: By Appointment *Only*.

When Peg returns to Madame Snootella's fourteen-weeks later for her appointment, she brings her mother. This isn't because she enjoys shopping with her mother. The last time she went shopping with her mother was in seventh grade, when Peg desperately wanted—no, *needed*—a pair of straight-legged, prewashed Levi's 501s, and somehow wound up leaving with a lacy Laura Ashley party dress. Peg brings her mother because the bride is *supposed* to bring her mother—especially if the bride has already shared the sensitive news that she has no intention of wearing the yellowed, mothball-tainted tablecloth her mother wore on *her* wedding day. The pair is admitted into the boutique on the first buzz.

"Welcome!" exclaims a noticeably less misanthropic Madam Snootella, rushing the door like an excited puppy dog. "You are so booooooooootiful!" She throws her arms around Peg's mother, and air-kisses both of her cheeks. Her mother points out that Peg is the one getting married. Madame then throws her arms around Peg, and air-kisses both of her cheeks. "You are even *more* booooooootiful!" she gushes.

But Peg isn't paying attention. She's completely overwhelmed by the racks of pure white *poof* that stretch out before her like nothing she has ever encountered at The Gap. Taking a deep breath, she introduces Snootella to the only friend who can protect her: Carolyn Bessette Kennedy, who is—as always—tastefully sheathed and folded into fourths in Peg's purse.

"Interesting," Snootella sniffs, snatching the page out of Peg's hand before disappearing into the stockroom.

Seconds later, Madame returns with six metric tons of beaded white taffeta that is so unruly, so unsheathlike, that it takes her and her entire staff of assistants to heave it out of the satin wheelbarrow in which they are transporting it. "Just try it on, sweetness." Snootella begs. "It will be so booooooootiful once it is on."

Of course, Peg couldn't "just try it on" even if she wanted to. The garment, like every garment in the boutique, is a size two, and Peg is not a size two. Yet. Before she even knows what's going on, she is whisked into a dressing room by Snootella's staff, where she's stripped down and strapped into a petticoat; restrained by ribbons, bound by bows, and poked with pins; fastened to a bustle; attached to a train; clamped to a headpiece. And once she is fully secured within the bridal apparatus, she waddles out of the dressing room, feeling like a giant piñata.

Her mother sheds a tear of joy. Madame Snootella applauds wildly. "You are so booooooootiful!" they shout together, wheeling her over to a three-panel mirror where the assistants are waiting beneath flattering overhead lights.

"You are a *princess* in this gown," one of them murmurs, gently patting Peg on the head. "A ray of sunshine," whispers another, gazing at her reflection in the mirror. An assistant to her right softly brushes Peg's hair. Another on her left sweetly massages her shoulders. *"We love you, Peg,"* they all seem to coo into her ear. *"We love you very much."*

Peg feels herself slipping under their spell, but deep down inside, she knows better. She knows these ladies do not really love her. She knows they do not think she is "boooooootiful." She knows that the second she walks out of Madam Snootella's Bridal Boutique, they're all going to high-five each other in the back room and merrily recount the day's events. "How 'bout that piñata in here this afternoon!" they are going to say.

The more Peg thinks about this, the more trapped she feels inside the monstrous restraining device. But just as she is about to flee back into the dressing room to trade her shackles for a sheath, Madam Snootella lays a delicate velvet pedestal at her feet.

We love you, Peg.

The assistants hold her hand to help her up.

We love you very much.

And suddenly, from this new altitude, a force stronger than Peg takes over—a familiar force she has come to know as her Inner Bride. As if by reflex, she finds herself sucking in her gut and balancing on her tiptoes. She smooths her giant hoop skirt and admires the Little Bo Peep bow on her butt. And as she stands there, studying her reflection in the mirror, she is overcome with the one thought she has been repressing since the day she bought that bridal magazine at CVS: *Oh my God, I'm really getting married.*

For a moment Peg wonders what Carolyn Bessette Kennedy would say if she saw her all dolled up in this poofy affair. But all that comes out of her mouth is one simple sentence.

"Excuse me," she begins. "Can I try this on with the rhinestone-studded tiara?"

A Tuxedo Tale: The Case of "Stan"

Stan looks in the Yellow Pages under "Rentals." Stan visits Mr. Fancypants. Stan gets measured, Stan gets married, Stan returns tux to Mr. Fancypants.

Fashion Answers for Grooms

Q: What is the difference between renting and owning a tuxedo?

A: The former entails renting under your real name and returning the tux after use; the latter entails renting under an assumed name and keeping the tux after use.

Q: If a white gown symbolizes that the bride is a virgin, what does a colored tux symbolize?

A: *Periwinkle blue*—symbolizes that you are an acne-prone adolescent headed for the junior prom and a future career as a cruise ship entertainer.

Purple crushed velvet—symbolizes that you are a pimp named "Papa Cool" who is wanted in twelve states for heroin trafficking.

Madras—symbolizes that you are going to be stranded at the altar.

Q: What are the five steps of tying a bow tie?

A: 1. Place tie around neck with one end hanging ⅝ inch lower than other, tie both ends into looped square knot, bend each end in front, pull first end three-quarters through not, pull second end halfway through knot, pull and tighten looped ends to adjust.
2. Repeat one million times.
3. Discontinue upon fashioning standard "noose knot"

and finding self standing on chair beneath ceiling rafter.

4. Step down; loosen tie from throat; resume normal breathing.
5. Secure crappy clip-on from nearest bellboy.

Fashion Answers for Brides

Q: How many fittings should I expect to have if my gown needs alterations?

A: Expect one fitting per pound of body weight. For example, if you weigh 130 pounds, expect to go on 130 fittings. This gives the seamstress the time she needs to make your gown too small and too large 130 times at a rate of $130/hour.

Q: Why isn't my fiancé supposed to see the gown until the day of the wedding?

A: Because he doesn't care.

What the Mother of the Bride Wears

Anything that makes her look better than the mother of the groom.

What the Mother of the Groom Wears

Anything that makes her look better than the mother of the bride.

What the Father of the Bride Wears

Anything with very deep pockets.

What the Father of the Groom Wears

Whatever.

From Nearly-wed
to Newlywed

The Nearly-weddings

....

Understanding the Shower

As we begin our analysis of the bridal shower, let me pause to remind you that I am of the male ilk and hence have no idea what actually goes on at one of these things. What better time, then, to fall back on our fictional case-study bride "Peg," who—though clearly an indispensable humor device—is clearly *not* based on my lovely, nonfictional bride, Meg.

As we've learned, Peg approaches just about everything concerning her wedding with mixed feelings—her own vs. her Inner Bride's. Here's where the two of them stand on the subject of showers:

PEG: You know what? It would be perfectly fine with me to skip this whole shower thing. I mean, I already dragged everyone out to our engagement party, then they're gonna have to spend more money getting all the way out

to the wedding and buying us *another* gift, and now I'm
supposed to ask them all to sacrifice *another* Saturday for
some dumb *bridal shower* to celebrate me even more? People would rather chew on lightbulbs than go to showers.
Why would I ever force anyone to have one for ME?

PEG'S INNER BRIDE (In soothing southern accent): There,
there, Sugarplum Peaches, of *course* y'all are gonna have
yourself a showah. Why, think of how down*hearted* you'd
be if none of your best girlfriends had the common courtesy to throw you a proper party. Darlin', do I need to
remind you that you spent most every weekend last July
makin' sure you got your pretty little button-nosed self
to every single one of *their* weddin' showahs? Now, you
listen to *me*, PeggySueSweetheartFairyPrincessPumpkin-
PuddinPie: You *deserve* to have a little ole showah you
can call your own. Because, babydoll, I do believe it's
payback time.

The Power of the Shower

It should come as no surprise that Peg soon found herself
the center of something that definitely didn't feel like a
normal social event. It felt like a grown-up version of a
birthday tea party, where all her little friends and all her
mommy's big friends brought her presents, shared cookies,
and made believe they wouldn't rather be chewing on
lightbulbs. Don't be surprised if you experience a similar

self-consciousness when it's *your* turn, especially once everyone starts engaging in that bizarre set of behaviors my sources classify as . . .

Totally Queer Shower Customs

1. All the guests surround the bride in a circle formation, stare at her, and repeat the phrases, *"Ooooh"* and *"Ahhh"* as she desperately searches for new and different ways of saying, "What a lovely salad spinner!" For example:

- *OOOOH*
  "What a *remarkable* salad spinner!"
- *AHHH*
  "Oh, look! Another *attractive produce rotation device!*
- *AAAUGHHH!!!*
  "Someone call 911! Peg is chewing on a lightbulb!

2. One guest lands the high-profile job of Shower Stenographer. It is her duty to keep meticulous records of which guest gave which salad spinner, so the bride doesn't accidentally send a thank-you note that reads: *Dear Grandma Mavis, thank you so much for the crotchless panties you got me that say "Cum and Get It Baby." How did you know that papaya is Stan's favorite flavor?*

3. A few guests do things with the ribbons and bows that all the salad spinners were wrapped in, such as fastening them to a paper plate, which the bride is supposed to save or put on her head or use as a bouquet or something. No one actually knows for sure.

4. Certain guests choose to engage in fun-filled activities such as "Guess the Number of Jelly Beans in the Jar" or "Pin the Phallus on the Groom."[25]

Specialty Showers

THE OFFICE SHOWER

This beloved occasion allows your colleagues to celebrate the day they'll no longer have to do your work while you spend company time planning your menu, fighting with your family, and not inviting your colleagues to your *real* shower.

THE THEME SHOWER

Ideal for the bride who finds herself becoming weirdly traditional the closer she gets to her Happiest Day. Request a "kitchen shower" if you've grown fascinated by mixing and toasting implements; a "linen shower" if you've developed an abnormal fixation with 300-thread-count damask pillowcases; and a "lingerie shower" if you're not too em-

---

[25] Note: Generally not the real groom.

barrassed to return twenty-three chain-mail teddies to the Cum and Get It catalog.[26]

THE JACK AND JILL

The co-ed couple's shower is sharply discouraged for any bride who wants to keep her fiancé around until the wedding itself. The only acceptable co-ed couple's shower is the kind that's conducted under a stream of hot water in the bathroom.

THE BACHELORETTE PARTY

A favorite among gals who find male stag parties so juvenile, so vulgar, so demeaning, they are forced to have one themselves. Party antics include dressing up in toilet paper wedding gowns, engaging in adult-themed scavenger hunts, and stuffing dollar bills down the athletic supporters of gyrating Chippendales dancers. Postparty antics include Breathalyzer tests, stomach pumpings, and court appearances.

Bachelor Parties: The Naked Truth

If you're a Nearly-wed groom, you probably think your bachelor party is a chance to go out with the boys for one

[26] in exchange for one jar of papaya body paint

last night of boozing, strip-clubbing, and fraternizing with professional women who just happen to be named Sugar or Chestitty. And you're right! Except . . .

1. You're not the type of guy who has *ever* gone out with the boys for a night of boozing, strip-clubbing, and fraternizing with professional women who just happen to be named Sugar or Chestitty.

2. If you *are* the type of guy who goes out for nights like these, you'll probably keep going out for them long after your bachelor party is through.[27]

For the sake of flattery, let's assume you fall into the first category. Let's say you're one of those "enlightened" brand of guys. Let's say you're engaged to Gloria Steinem. Let's say the kind of bachelor party you had in mind was just a few rounds of pool at the tavern down the block, or a weekend camping trip with a couple of close friends, or a gentlemanly dinner at the best steak house in town.

And now, let's quit kiddin' yourself, pal.

Let's just admit that no matter how "enlightened" you are, you secretly feel that the kind of bachelor party you should *really* be having isn't the kind that involves camping, filet mignon, or a few rounds of eight ball. It's' the kind that involves boozing, strip-clubbing, and fraternizing with professional women who just happen to be named Sugar or Chestitty. And if you *don't* feel this way[28], you can be

[27] and your divorce is final
[28] liar

sure that at least one of your buddies does. Typically this buddy still goes by a nickname he's had since junior high, such as Chunks, which he got that night he slept in the toilet after polishing off a magnum of Harvey's Bristol Cream he swiped from his parents' liquor cabinet. Chunks has spent every weekend since he was nine-and-a-half going to bachelor parties. He's not just a "party person," he's a "*bachelor* party person," and hell if yours is going to be the first one where he sits around with a bunch of Nancy-boys being "enlightened."

And so it is that about a week before your wedding, you find yourself crammed around the minibar of a chauffeur-driven SUV, singing "Freebird" with a group of your best bachelor pals, only two of whom have actually met before, and only one of whom is actually a bachelor (Chunks). But you're not gonna let *that* spoil the fun on your last night out with the boys, are ya, boss? Heck no! Already you've been chauffeured off to Buckets O' Buffalo Wings, It's The Balls Paintball Palace on Route 3A, and Big Wedgie's House of Foozball, where you all got kicked out after Chunks challenged that Cub Scout troop to a head-butting match. And are you ever having fun! Oh, sure, your eye-balls are spinning around a little from those Jaegermeister and Cuervo beer bong funnel shooters the boys have been plying you with all night, and yeah, maybe you *will* need some minor knee-replacement surgery if you keep tripping over that bowling ball and chain they locked to your ankle at the start of the night's merriment, but hell: This is *your last night out with the boys,* and by God, you're going to enjoy it.

Woo-hoo! Now you're smoking a cigar! High five! Now you're exchanging risqué jokes! Roll down the window and chuck another bottle at the Stop sign, baby, 'cause you're in a runaway Wrangler headed for that Holiday Inn on Stag Street where *anything* goes: Videos that are X-rated! (Par-TAY!) A game of poker! (Sweet!) A pair of pissed-off chambermaids who barge into the room threatening to have you evicted for violating noise pollution code #147-Y (Uh-oh!).

But wait just a second, buddy boy! The name tag on that one maid says "Sugar!" And the one on that other maid says "Chestitty!" And what exactly is Sugar doing with those candied yams she seems to be spreading all over Chestitty's . . . YOWZA! Can it be? Is it true? You bet your bachelorhood it's true, you old dog! Why, Sugar and Chestitty aren't chambermaids at all, they're . . . *strippers!* And now they're coming at YOU, tying you to the chair with their lacy little aprons; unbuckling your belt with their rubber dishwashing gloves; feather-dusting you in places you've never been feather-dusted before.

All around, everyone is hootin' and howlin' in a testosterone delirium that makes you feel flush; makes you feel dizzy; makes you feel like it's New Year's Eve and no one is really having a good time but everyone is pretending to because everyone thinks that what you're supposed to do on New Year's Eve is par-TAY, dude, even though what everyone would *rather* do, more than *anything,* is stay home with the most beautiful, perfect woman with whom they are very much in love and with whom they are going to spend the rest of their lives so they will never again have to spend another night tied to a chair at a Holiday Inn with a feather duster down their pants while a grown man named Chunks stands over them watching the whole thing with a stupid grin on his face that seems to alternate between plain old goofy and downright scary.

When you awaken from your alcohol coma the next afternoon, you scratch your head and survey the scene: a yam-encrusted Holiday Inn room; Chunks, plastered with luggage tags and sleeping in the toilet; a yak.[29] "So this was my last night out with the boys," you think, a wistful grin spreading across your lips. "Thank *God* I'm getting married."

[29] wearing go-go boots

The Conjugal Countdown

....

One Week to Wedded Bliss

Most couples spend their final week as Nearly-weds developing an intimate relationship with the Acu-Weather Five-Day Forecast. Will it rain? Will it snow? And how is that low-pressure storm system brewing over the Republic of Ibugakk going to affect the lighting for your outdoor candids?

Relax. As the week goes on, you'll stop obsessing together. You'll start obsessing alone. If you're the bride, you'll find yourself fixating on something that will make you feel comfortable with your role as Epicenter of Attention: yourself. If you're the groom, you'll find yourself exerting maniacal control over something—*anything*—that will make you feel like you *have* a role in the wedding you'll be attending the following week.

See the following schedule:

Official Obsessive-Compulsive Countdown

Bride's One-Week Countdown

- lose 97 pounds
- get hair highlighted
- get hair lowlighted
- get hair permed
- get hair straightened
- lose 47 pounds
- get facial
- get face lift
- lose 15 pounds
- get eyelashes tinted
- get teeth capped
- get breast-reduction surgery (left)
- get breast enhancement surgery (left)
- lose 3.42 pounds
- go to gym
- go to tanning salon
- go to spa
- get seaweed wrap treatment
- get aromatherapy treatment
- get psychotherapy treatment

Groom's One-Week Countdown

- call to confirm make of limo rental
- call to confirm price of limo rental
- cancel limo
- wash and wax car
- Simonize car
- Midasize car
- deodorize car
- redeodorize car
- call to reserve new limo
- inspect new limo
- check mileage
- check fluid levels
- check Blue Book value
- interview chauffeur
- give chauffeur written driving test
- give chauffeur parallel-parking test
- give chauffeur drug test
- request new chauffeur
- request new limo
- request to be freed from trunk of limo

One Day to Wedded Bliss

All you have to do now is cross off any minor details left on your six-skazillion "to-do" lists, such as "get marriage license." This is done by visiting your local town hall to certify that you're not marrying your brother or sister, and you don't have a communicable disease. If you *are* marrying your brother or sister, and you do have a communicable disease, don't bother visiting your local town hall. Visit a town hall in Northern Appalachia, where these traits are mandatory requirements for marriage.

One Night to Wedded Bliss

Save this date for your rehearsal dinner, a custom intended to make sure the groom's family pays for *something*. The point of the rehearsal dinner is to *rehearse* not getting too trashed the following day. If you want to be fresh as a couple of daisies at your wedding, you won't drink like a couple of sailors at your rehearsal dinner.

Following the rehearsal dinner, it is customary for Nearly-weds to meet their out-of-town friends at a seedy tavern and booze it up like sailors until dawn.

One Hour to Wedded Bliss

The final hour is traditionally reserved for taking leave of your faculties. To prepare for *your* last-minute meltdown, let's catch up with our fictional case-study Nearly-weds "Stan" and "Peg," who are *still* in no way based upon me, Dan, and my nonfictional bride, Meg.

With just an hour to go, Peg is ensconced in her spacious dressing room, surrounded by her minions: the attendants, the hairdresser, the makeup artist, the photographer, the videographer, the production crew from "Entertainment Tonight," the throngs of autograph-seekers shouting, "All hail Peg! All hail Peg!" etc. She's queen of the court, belle of the ball, and all at once it hits her: "The *pillow!*" she shrieks. "What did we do with that little satin pillow the ring bearer is supposed to hold??!"

Meanwhile, Stan is in the men's room down the hall, alone, wondering if he should wear the black bow tie or the blue bow tie. He got the black one free with the tux, but he bought the blue one a few weeks later, privately, as kind of a backup bow tie. "The black one is definitely the safe one," Stan reasons. "But the blue one will make it clear that I am the groom." He holds the blue one up to the bathroom mirror. He holds the black one up to the bathroom mirror. "I wonder what a red bow tie would look like with this getup," he wonders.

"SOMEBODY FIND ME THAT FREAKING PIL-LOW!!" Peg is now screaming hysterically at her bridesmaids. She's rummaging through her bags, tearing apart the room, hurling couch cushions at the Maid of Honor. "Where the hell is Stan?!" she shouts. "Maybe *Stan* has the pillow! I need STAN! I NEED THAT PILLOW!!" She rushes the door, knocking down everyone in her way. "The PILLOW, Stan!" she wails, running half-naked down the hallway. "We can't get married if we don't find that PILLLLLLOWWWWWWW!!!!"

"Hal Lichtenstein wore a blue bow tie at *his* wedding," Stan recalls, "but Hal could wear gingham and get away with it. On me, the blue one looks kinda cheesy. But the black one makes me look like a parking valet. Maybe I could wear the black one for the ceremony and the blue one at the reception. No. The black one during the reception and the blue one for the ceremony. NO! Just the black one. No! Just the blue one. Hmm . . . what about both at once?"

Stan's hands are trembling. His face starts sweating. *"Peg!"* he finally cries out, lunging for the bathroom door-knob. "I NEED YOU! *Blue tie or black tie?!"*

But as he darts out of the bathroom to hunt her down, Stan is tackled by a deranged, half-naked woman with tears of mascara streaming down her cheeks, barreling down the hallway like a lunatic, shouting something about . . . a pillow? Tumbling to the ground, they land on top of each other, startled into silence. For a second, it reminds them both of that time on the beach when everyone decided to play full-contact Capture the Flag. It was last summer, before they got engaged. Before they got into that fight over the seating arrangement, and that other one over the photography, and those fifty-three others over the food. Before they ever turned into the kind of couple who cared just a little too much about small satin pillows and black or blue bow ties. And slowly, a sense of perspective returns to Peg and Stan. They're not crazy, just nervous, that's all. And as they lie huddled together on the hallway floor, neither one has ever felt more certain of what they're going to do as soon as they get up. They're going to elope.

Just kidding!! Of course they're not going to elope! They're going to have a wedding! Because after all the worrying, all the anticipating, all the writing of the nonrefundable deposit checks, they know—just as *you'll* know an hour before *your* wedding—that there is no escape from . . .

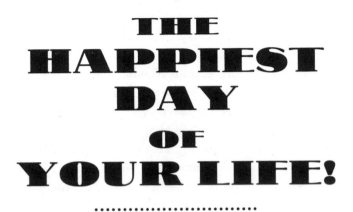

THE HAPPIEST DAY OF YOUR LIFE!

....

Step One: The Processional

It used to be that the bride's father would "give her away," symbolizing that she had become too much of a financial drain during the months preceding the wedding. If you're a modern bride who finds this practice sexist, tell your patriarchal oppressor you won't let yourself be "given away." For a mutually agreed upon fee, however,[30] you'll be happy to let him walk you down the aisle.

---

[30] For example: the outstanding balance on the florist

Step Two: The Vows

It has become increasingly popular for Nearly-weds to write their own vows, a process that entails plagiarizing vows written by other couples, inserting your own names, and telling everyone, "We wrote the whole thing ourselves." By personalizing your vows, you can avoid saying anything you find old-fashioned, like "love, honor, and obey" or "I do."

Step Three: The Reading

Many Nearly-weds wish to incorporate a poem or passage that has always been special to them, a custom that usually results in the depressing discovery that they do not have a poem or passage that has always been special to them. In the end they find themselves settling for such classics as *A Treasury of Wedding Haiku,* by Loretta Spittle, because *The Prophet,* by Kahlil Gibran, has been checked out of the library until the year 12,000 by other Nearly-weds who had to round up something to read.

To eliminate this inconvenience, I have personally scoured through the great wedding readings of our time and condensed them into one all-encompassing, easy-to-read classic. Why not rip this page out of the book right now and present it to the victim you're forcing to read at *your* ceremony?

ALL-PURPOSE WEDDING READING
BY DAN ZEVIN[31]

We're together, we're independent
we're the same, we're not the same
we're one, we're two
love, love, love
blah
*   blah*
*   blah*
Amen.

Step Four: The Exchange of Rings

The wedding ring is a symbol of your decision to spend all of eternity with one person you've chosen over all others. It's no wonder that many Nearly-weds develop a violent, shaking palsy in their hands when it comes time to actually exchange these rings. Fortunately, this condition is tempo-

---

[31] Nom de plume: Loretta Spittle

rary. The instant you finally manage to jam the rings onto each other's fingers, your hands will steady and you'll develop an overwhelming sense of tranquillity and well-being. This is also no wonder, since you've now begun spending all of eternity with the one person you've chosen over all others.

Step Five: The Kiss

Since this is the part your guests have *really* been waiting for, the pressure is on to give them a deep, passionate kiss that will leave them hooting, "Take it all off!" When you're done, give your mate a kiss as well.

Reception Recreation

....

And Now, the Fun Part

Once the ceremony is over,[32] you're going to experience an ecstatic, delirious, supreme sensation of euphoria. You're going to be so transfixed with joy that all you'll be able to do is prop yourself up between your spouse and your parents for that out-of-body experience we call . . .

A Receiving Line

The challenge of a receiving line is to sustain your adorable, toothy grin until such time as you "feel the burn" in your lip muscles. Known as the Receiving Line Smile (RLS), this isometric exercise serves a dual function: (1) It allows

[32] and your medication wears off

your well-wishers to see how much you enjoy being vigorously hugged and kissed by them, and (2) it allows you to talk ventriloquist-style to your parents so you can find out each of their names.

The Dance of Fear

The thought of taking the spotlight for a solo dance performance strikes terror into the hearts of most Nearly-weds, especially those who haven't spent the last six months taking fox-trot classes at the Fred Astaire Institute. The good news is that the first dance usually takes the spotlight *off* the two of you. Traditionally, the bride's father cuts in to dance with the bride, the bride's mother cuts in to dance with the groom, the groom's father cuts in to dance with the bride's cousin, the caterer cuts in to dance with the florist, the priest cuts in to dance with the ring bearer, and before you know it, the two of you will be gliding off the dance floor and cha-cha-cha–ing over to the bar. This is the ideal spot to rest your twinkle toes and . . .

Prepare to Get Toasted

Following the first dance, certain preselected guests will give a toast in your honor, a tradition whereby they punish you for making them engage in public speaking. This is an excellent time to place a couple of shopping bags over your heads and remove all sharp implements from the table. Then just sit back and laugh politely as you're exalted in the following fashion:

1. The toastmaster starts off with a lie.

Example: "I was so pleased and excited when Stan and Peg asked me to make a toast."

2. The toastmaster recalls a poignant anecdote about the bride.

Example: "I shall never forget the night she slept with the entire JV cross-country team and still had energy left to steal that UPS truck and light the Dairy Queen on fire."

3. The toastmaster recalls a poignant anecdote about the groom.

Example: "Well, I guess everyone already knows how he wet the bed until he was sixteen. But now let me tell you about the time he got sent away to that camp for over-weight children after the kids started calling him 'Stan-Stan-Fattyman.' "

4. The toastmaster wishes the couple a long and happy life together.

Example: "Stan, Peg, a lot of people in this room give your marriage a month, tops, but I have a feeling you'll stay together at least until the baby is born."

5. The toastmaster concludes with a sentiment that brings everyone to tears.

Example: "And now I'd like to turn the microphone over to

one of the seventy-three other people who'd like to propose a toast. Great-granddad Ulysses, why don't we start with you . . ."

Mixing, Mingling, and Being Socially Retarded

Throughout the reception, you'll be expected to circulate jauntily through the crowd, charming everyone with your sparkling conversation and witty badinage. Here is a typical discussion:

GUEST: So how does it feel to be married?
YOU: (grunt) Me so happy. Me married. Yes, yes. Happy married.

Notice how attending your own reception temporarily disables the cranial lobe controlling the mingle reflex. Several factors cause this common affliction:

Mingle Inhibitor 1. *The overwhelming sensation of seeing everyone from your entire life in the same room.*
By the bar, you spot your junior high prom date talking to your fiancé's grandfather. At the far corner, you see your old boss. At the opposite corner, you see your new boss who just fired him. Look! There's your radical lesbian

friend from Ann Arbor! Hey! Here comes nutty Uncle Alfonse with the dirty jokes!

Mingle Inhibitor 2. *The overwhelming realization that you are responsible for everyone in this room having fun.*
Why aren't Mr. and Mrs. Flynn line-dancing? Why isn't cousin Gwyneth eating her fruit cup? Why is your radical lesbian friend from Ann Arbor kick-boxing Uncle Alfonse in the groin?

Mingle Inhibitor 3. *The invisible fence.*
The invisible fence is a strange psychological barrier that prevents many guests from approaching you at all on the Happiest Day of Your Life. These guests figure that you're already overwhelmed by (a) seeing everyone from your entire lives in the same room and (b) realizing that you're responsible for everyone in this room having fun. Therefore, they go out of their way to make sure they don't talk to you, doing everything in their power to ignore you completely and treat you as if you don't exist. They do this to be polite.

How to Mix, Mingle, and Not Be Socially Retarded

The simplest way to make sure you talk to all your guests is by "table hopping," otherwise known as "running around to every table and answering the question 'So how does it feel to be married?' several killionmillion times." For efficiency's sake, approach each table at the precise moment when everyone has food stuffed into their mouths. Then, say: "Hello, guests! It feels great to be married! Oops, better go see Table Two, see ya!"

The Most Significant Cake of Your Life

Envision the moment: A mystical hush comes over the room as the much-ballyhooed wedding cake is transported on its sacred mobile display cart for all to behold. Your guests, drawn to the blinding white pastry by a force they cannot understand, huddle close, enraptured, to witness that once-in-a-lifetime sight of two individuals cutting some cake. Don't destroy the sanctity of the slicing by grinding the cake childishly into each other's faces. It's more mature to take turns spoonfeeding each other. This symbolizes that you love each other enough to share a life together. And don't forget that you're supposed to save a piece to share on your first anniversary. This symbolizes that you love each other enough to share a crystallized, freezer-burned lump that's been buried under an ice-cube tray and a Lean Cuisine for the past year.

Getting Off (on) the Garter

After dessert, it is customary to thank those assembled by performing a soft-core sex show. This is done with the tender and beautiful garter ceremony, in which you send your guests into an orgiastic frenzy by simulating public foreplay. Here's how: With a little romantic trombone music in the background, assume the standard matrimony position: the bride on top, perched regally on her throne; the groom on his hands and knees below her. The groom then begins his search for the bride's garter (or "G") spot:

1. The groom fondles the bride's inner thigh, searching for her G spot.
2. The groom fondles the bride's six-layer slip, searching for her G spot.
3. The groom fondles the bride's inner petticoat lining attached to the corselette straps fastened to the six-layer slip, searching for her G spot.
4. The bride loses patience and guides the groom's hand straight to her G spot.
5. The encounter reaches climax as the groom slides the garter down the bride's thigh—orally or manually—and exposes it to a crowd screaming in ecstasy.

Once the groom has finished his business with the garter, he casts it off to a crowd of bachelors who've been told they'll be next to get married if they catch it.

The garter generally lands on the floor.

The Luck of the Toss: Bouquet-Throwing Tips

The bouquet *never* lands on the floor, but many of the women vying to catch it do. This is because they've been beaten unconscious by a crowd of savagely competitive bachelorettes who've been told they'll be next to get married if they catch it.

To reduce emergency room costs, brides should plan ahead. Several months before the wedding, choose a training partner at random, such as the unattached friend you're most eager to marry off. Meet at the reception site each day for a rigorous game of catch, pitching a bouquet over and over until your partner could catch it blindfolded. When your Happiest Day finally arrives, don't take any risks. Implant a powerful magnet inside your flowers and her baseball mitt. Hire a team of heavily armed front men to surround her portable stepladder. Then just twirl around and toss your bouquet to the wind. (Remember, no playing favorites!) Whichever bachelorette happens to be in the right place at the right time will be the next lucky Nearly-wed!

Why the Divorce Rate Is Over 50 Percent

When the garter and bouquet toss are through, the gent who caught the garter places it on the lass who caught the bouquet. This signifies that they will get married to each other.

Escaping Unscathed

Just before the party's over, both of you must change into something practical for your grand getaway, such as helmets, padded crash-test dummy suits, and protective safety goggles. This snappy ensemble is ideal for those occasions when you expect to be gang-pelted with rock-hard granules of rice. It's equally well suited for those occasions when you expect to be riding in an automobile fully loaded with shaving cream, tin cans, and Just Married signage festively obstructing the driver's field of vision.

Consummating the Modern Marriage

It would be archaic to think your wedding night will be the first time the two of you engage in intimate relations. More likely, it'll be the first time you won't. Fatigued by your strenuous wedding workout, you'll be lucky if you have enough energy to stagger into the bridal boudoir, floss, and take a swig of Maalox before snoring yourselves into a catatonic stupor. Consummating your union in this fashion is an excellent initiation into life as a married couple.

Honeymoon, Here We Come!

....

Getting the Most Out of Your Vacation

Your honeymoon is a time to rest, to recuperate, to experience the phenomenon of everyone being uncharacteristically nice to you as soon as they find out the news.

YOU: Excuse me, stewardess, do you think you could tape this window shut when you get a minute?

STEWARDESS: What do I look like, a carpenter?

YOU: I am on my honeymoon.

STEWARDESS: *HONEYMOON?!* Hey, Muriel, we've got a couple of adorable honeymooners in six A and B! Right this way to first class, folks. Our captain will be landing momentarily to expedite your upgrade to the Concorde SST. Caviar, anyone?

Clearly, the trick to getting the most out of your honeymoon[33] is to make sure everyone knows you're on it. Hold hands at all times. Sport lapel pins that say: ASK US IF WE'RE ON OUR HONEYMOON! Wear your wedding gown and tux to the beach.

Where to Honeymoon

The honeymoon spot is usually chosen by the groom, explaining why many couples end up in supersophisticated topless resorts with names like Lake Titty-Cockah. In the event that these places are overbooked, choose amongst the popular "Lovebirds" packages that follow:

THE SEA CRUISE

HONEYMOON HOT SPOTS

Bahamas, Caribbean, ocean floor

ROMANTIC RECREATION

consuming own body weight during midnight buffet; hurling self overboard during musical revue

TRAVELING COMPANIONS

near-death bingo enthusiasts wearing Hawaiian leis, life support equipment

HONEYMOON SUITE

casket-sized cabin with saltwater-logged carpet

---

[33] the most complimentary rum punch cocktails, the most complimentary salad bar visits, the most complimentary hotel-room fruit baskets . . .

COMPLIMENTARY SOUVENIR

commemorative sea-sickness bag from Infirmary Deck vomitorium

THE EXOTIC ADVENTURE

HONEYMOON HOT SPOTS

Costa Rican jungle, Serengeti Plain, emergency inoculation clinic

ROMANTIC RECREATION

rafting the white water; tracking the wildebeests; fleeing the insurgent cannibal terrorists

TRAVELING COMPANIONS

indestructible Australian backpackers wielding beer-stained *Lonely Planet* travel guides

HONEYMOON SUITE

wind-resistant canvas walls; natural dirt floors

COMPLIMENTARY SOUVENIR

encephalitis

CAMP KITSCH

HONEYMOON HOT SPOTS

Dollywood, Niagara Falls, Las Vegas, Poconos, Graceland, Mall of America

ROMANTIC RECREATION

taking kooky pictures of each other with "real people" at authentic tourist traps

TRAVELING COMPANIONS

overeducated hipness victims who did masters thesis on postmodern irony; corn-dog eaters

HONEYMOON SUITE

wacky heart-shaped tub, nutty heart-shaped bed, tireless heart-shaped couple engaging in high-volume sex next door

COMPLIMENTARY SOUVENIR

tacky tin ashtray stolen from hotel for collection

THE EURO-JAUNT

HONEYMOON HOT SPOTS

Paris, London, Rome, lost luggage counter

ROMANTIC RECREATION

wandering aimlessly around historical district in search of historical district

TRAVELING COMPANIONS

American exchange students in Hard Rok Café shirts and EuroDisney mouse ears; traveling gypsy pickpockets

HONEYMOON SUITE

separate bunk beds in asbestos-ridden basement referred to as "charming pensione" in brochure

COMPLIMENTARY SOUVENIR

twenty-seven pounds of loose foreign change worth approx. .014 cents

THE HOME-STAY

HONEYMOON HOT SPOTS

current mailing address

ROMANTIC RECREATION
>   sleeping in, eating out, opening gifts, making love, dancing in pajamas

TRAVELING COMPANIONS
>   each other, forever

HONEYMOON SUITE
>   bedroom, living room, shower, kitchen table, ironing board . . .

COMPLIMENTARY SOUVENIR
>   see "traveling companions"

The Honeymoon Is Over
(A Play in One Ring)

SCENE: An adorable couple, "Stan" and "Peg"—who, even at this late date, are in no way based on me, Dan, and my adorable bride, Meg—are just returning to their apartment from their fabulous honeymoon vacation, where they received many complimentary souvenirs. Before they even get the chance to put down their luggage and remove their lapel pins that say ASK US IF WE'RE ON OUR HONEYMOON!, the PHONE rings.

PHONE: *Ringggggggg*
PEG: Hello?
PEG'S NEW MOTHER-IN-LAW: Hello honey and how was your little trip . . . good, listen—my closest and dearest

friend, Lucille Schnitzer, is very concerned that you didn't get the thoughtful and expensive serving platter she sent for your wedding gift. Did you get it did you get it did you get it did you get it did you get it did you—

PEG: Stan, it's for you.

STAN: Hi, Ma.

STAN'S MOTHER: Stanley! Mrs. Schnitzer is *beside* herself about the priceless antique platter she had shipped to you. She's had a trace put on it by the UPS, the FBI, the CIA . . . and still nothing. Is there *any* way you may have overlooked it?

STAN: When did she send it?

STAN'S MOTHER: Yesterday.

STAN: Ma, we just walked in the door from Lake Titty-Cockah! What makes her think we didn't get it?

STAN'S MOTHER: She never got a thank-you note. What is she *supposed* to think?

A Thank-You Note Tutorial

....

The Three Types of Thank-You Notes

1. The Thank-You Note the Groom Sends:

Dear Mrs. Schnitzer,
                    Thanks for the, um, thing.
                                        Your friend, Stan

(actual size)

2. The Thank-You Note the Bride Sends:

My Dearest Schnitzers,

How can I ever express my heartfelt gratitude for the lovely Lucite serving platter you so thoughtfully bestowed upon Stan and me for our Happiest Day. The decorative porcelain aardvarks adorning the imitation wooden handles are lovely, as is the lovely spiderweb motif (complete with detailed larvae!) etched right into the surface. Whenever Stan and I gaze at our lovely new platter, it reminds us of our favorite creatures in nature, the aardvark and the spider egg. And I must commend you on the lovely color scheme of the platter as well! I didn't even know Lucite came in such a lovely fusion of burnt orange and aquamarine! Truly lovely. It is absolutely the loveliest gift we received, and you are both lovely.

Lovingly,
Peg and Stan

3. The Thank-You Note the Bride and Groom Would Both Like to Send But Don't:

> Dear Mr. and Mrs. Schnitzer,
>
> Thanks a lot for the grotesque aardvark and spiderweb monstrosity you unloaded on us—we can't wait to return it for cash! It was truly thoughtful of you to leave the price tag from Lucite Liquidators on it so we'll know where our next $3.99 is coming from. And how clever of you to wrap it up in that fancy box from Neiman-Marcus! We'd love to have you over for dinner soon so we can act like we use your sickening serving tray all the time.
>
> Don't hold your breath,
Peg and Stan

The All-New, Totally Married You

....

What to Change Your Name To

The issue of postnuptial nomenclature leaves many brides confused by all their options. Some will keep their own name, some will take their groom's name, some will hyphenate their maiden name and their married name, some will combine the first part of their maiden name and the second part of their married name to create an all-new-and-improved hybrid name,[34] some will lose a consonant, some will buy a vowel, some will solve the puzzle, and some will take the rest on gift certificate.

To simplify matters, the bride and groom should *both* change their names—to something that will get their wedding announcement on the society pages of newspapers nationwide.

---

[34] such as O'Silverstein

*How to Get Your Wedding Announcement
on the Society Pages
of Newspapers Nationwide*

Mix and match from the categories below:

Suggested Names

BRIDE: Blaine / Jacqueline / Imelda
   DuPONT / HEARST / VANDERBILT
GROOM: John-John / F. Scott / Winston
    CARNEGIE / KENNEDY / GETTY

Recommended Residences

BRIDE: affluent East Coast suburb
GROOM: charming West Coast city

Favored Wedding Sites

CEREMONY: historical house of worship
RECEPTION: estate of close personal friend

Appropriate Occupations

BRIDE: publishing / advertising / president of socially responsible nonprofit organization

GROOM: medicine / law / president of multibillion-dollar investment banking organization

Preferred Parents

MOTHERS: museum trustees / philanthropists / animal lovers[35]

FATHERS: monarchs / politicians / deceased

Acceptable Site of Future Home

Large East Coast city
Large West Coast city
Affluent suburb of Chicago
Vague yet impressive international locale

Menu

Not chicken

[35] figuritively speaking

The Winning Wedding Announcement

DuHearsterbilt-Carnekennegetty

Blaine Jacquelda DuHearsterbilt of Greenwich, CT (formerly Stacie Shapiro of Secaucus, NJ), and Sir John-John F. Scottston Carnekennegetty XI, M.D. Esq., of San Diego, CA (formerly Eddie Sigliano of Detroit), were wed Saturday at the Sistine Chapel in Rome, Italy (formerly known as Brooklyn City Hall). Close personal friend and Supreme Pontiff Pope John Paul II performed the ceremony and hosted the reception on the patio of his Vatican home. The bride, editor-in-chief of the *New York Times* society page and creative director of the Ogilvey, Mather, DDB Saatchi & Saatchi advertising agency, is the president and founder of Girl Scouts. The groom, an orthopedic cardioneurosurgeon and attorney general of the United Nations, is the president and founder of Merrill Lynch and the great-grandson of Dean Witter. The bride's parents are His Royal Highness King Ferdinando Rothschild of Copenhagen, France, and the former Isabella "Sissy" Hemingway, a breeder of golden retriever show dogs. The groom's mother is Mamie Guggenheim Fulbright. His father, the former president of the United States, Thomas "Woodrow" Wilson, is presently deceased. The couple will divide their time between Boston, San Francisco, and vacation homes in the Americas before settling into their home in Winnetka, IL. Prime rib was served.

Nearly-wed
No More

Overcoming Wedding Withdrawal

It's been one week since their honeymoon, and our fictional case-study couple "Stan" and "Peg"—who have grown to resent your suspicion that they're based on me, Dan, and my nonfictional bride, Meg—are slumped across the futon in their darkened living room, surrounded by empty Pottery Barn boxes, staring blankly at the Styrofoam packing peanuts that litter the floor. By all accounts, they should be basking in the glory of their towering achievement. The ceremony was beautiful; the reception, a triumph. Stan's mother even made a rare complimentary remark about the food.[36]

And yet, their passage from Nearly-wed to Newlywed has been bittersweet. Back in the civilian world, Peg finds herself lunging for the office phone every time it rings, hoping it might be her old friend Guillermo the floríste, Klaus the photographer, or even that ninety-year-old non−

---

[36] Quote: "I like the color of these plates."

English-speaking seamstress from Madam Snootella's Bridal Boutique. But the voice on the other end always belongs to some chump asking to conduct business-related business.

For months, Peg was CEO of Nearly-wed Central, but now her life suddenly lacks purpose. Sure, she remembers the headaches, the hassles, the protracted nervous breakdown known as wedding planning. But in a weird way, she kind of misses it. The only thing that gets her through the day is the knowledge that as soon as she gets home, she'll slip on her veil and fall asleep in the flickering light of her wedding video.

As for Stan, he's also having trouble readjusting to the postnuptial world. All he can talk about is the wedding — reviewing it, rehashing it, speed-dialing everyone on the guest list and pressuring them into providing their own personal reflections. Lately he seems to get an answering machine no matter who he calls: *"Hi, we can't get to the phone right now. If this is Stan, yes, we had a good time at your wedding. Our favorite part was when you did the Chicken Dance. We also liked that poem by Loretta Spittle during the ceremony. Please stop asking us about it. Let go of it, Stan. Get on with your life. Please wait for the beep."*

But Stan can't get on with his life. He can't wait for the beep. He's so stuck in the faded memory of the Happiest Day of His Life, he's actually clinging to some pathetic pipe dream about — get this! — writing a whole *book* about it! The mind boggles.

Are You Suffering from Wedding Withdrawal?
Take This E-Z Quiz!

RESPONSE TEST FOR RECOVERING BRIDES

• I feel a profound sense of emptiness if the UPS guy does not arrive at my door with at least one box a day.
CONSTANTLY / INCESSANTLY / ALWAYS (circle one)

• I feel a codependent need to act as "wedding mentor" to anyone who is thinking of getting married.
CONSTANTLY / INCESSANTLY / ALWAYS

• I cannot control my reflex to reach for wedding magazines at the supermarket checkout lane.
CONSTANTLY / INCESSANTLY / ALWAYS

• I cannot *wait* to go to the next wedding I'm invited to.
CONSTANTLY / INCESSANTLY / ALWAYS

• I don't even care if I don't like the people getting married.
CONSTANTLY / INCESSANTLY / ALWAYS

• I don't even care if I'm not invited.
CONSTANTLY / INCESSANTLY / ALWAYS

• I believe that what everyone wants for the holidays this year is a framed copy of my wedding portrait.
CONSTANTLY / INCESSANTLY / ALWAYS

- I have dinner parties solely for the purpose of using my new flatwear.

  CONSTANTLY / INCESSANTLY / ALWAYS

- I serve everything in bowls at these parties.

  CONSTANTLY / INCESSANTLY / ALWAYS

- Once I even served a bowl of pizza.

  CONSTANTLY / INCESSANTLY / ALWAYS

RESPONSE TEST FOR RECOVERING GROOMS

- When I notice I've got this ring on my finger, it reminds me that I recently got married.

  ONCE / NEVER / RING?

A Basic Wedding Cessation Program

The first step to curing Wedding Withdrawal is admitting the truth to yourselves. Repeat after me: "THE WEDDING IS OVER." Say it loud, say it proud! "THE WEDDING IS *OVER!!*" The second step is seeking professional help. After all, only crazy people talk to themselves while reading books.

Chances are, you'll have to wait several decades before you get an appointment with a trained professional. Don't waste that time allowing Wedding Withdrawal to get the best of you. Instead, get right back in the swing of things and start planning for the future. Hey, your fiftieth anniversary party is right around the corner!